BATTERSEA
HERE FOR EVERY DOG AND CAT

A DOG A DAY

365 stories
of delightful
dogs to brighten
every single day

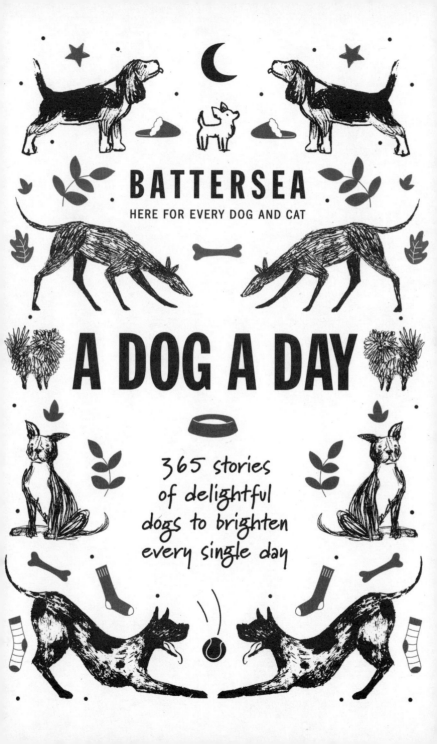

BATTERSEA

HERE FOR EVERY DOG AND CAT

A DOG A DAY

365 stories of delightful dogs to brighten every single day

CONTENTS

Battersea will always be here for every dog and cat, and has been since 1860.

Battersea takes dogs and cats in, gives them the expert care they need and finds them new homes that are just right for them.

They help pet owners make informed choices, provide training advice, and campaign for changes in the law. They also help other rescue centres and charities at home and abroad because they want to be here for every dog and cat, wherever they are, for as long as they need Battersea.

Your purchase will help Battersea continue its important work. Thank you.

JANUARY

1 JANUARY

Hershey

When the American actor Jeremy Renner was involved in an accident on New Year's Day in 2023 that saw him run over by his 6,350 kg (14,000lb) snow plough, his injuries landed him in intensive care, fighting for his life. Determined to recover, Jeremy, who plays Hawkeye in the smash hit Marvel films, faces many months on his path to rehabilitation – but he won't be making the journey alone. Just three months into that recovery, he posted a cute snap on Instagram of his Husky, Hershey, sitting on the end of his bed, calling her 'my little protector'.

2 JANUARY

Bertie

She was known as the Iron Lady, but the UK's first-ever female Prime Minister, Margaret Thatcher, had a huge soft spot for dogs and was photographed over the years with every type imaginable. It's been reported that in her dotage she would visit the local park just to fuss over the dogs she came across there. But one photograph, above all the others, really captures the joy she found in our four-legged friends, showing the former PM sitting on a bench with an Italian Greyhound called Bertie, who had jumped up onto her knee for a lick and a fuss. Bertie's owners said of the incident, 'being a typical Italian Greyhound, Bertie had made a beeline for a comfortable lap and she greeted him with delight.' On this day in 1988, Thatcher became the longest-serving prime minister of the twentieth century, passing H.H. Asquith.

3 JANUARY

Jewel, Ziggy, Zelda & Wozzie

Apple co-founder Steve Wozniak is an animal advocate, clearly loves dogs and has had many over the years, including one (Wozzie) named after him! His business partner, Steve Jobs, cared about animals enough to be a vegetarian but didn't like dogs in the workplace and banned them from the Apple campus. The two Steves incorporated Apple on this day in 1977 and at the time of its launch, in 1983, Steve W had three Siberian Huskies and an Australian Shepherd dog, along with another four of mixed breed.

Sage

The Doors, the hugely popular band who have sold 34 million albums worldwide, released their very first LP on this day in 1967. Their frontman, Jim Morrison, and his partner, Pamela Courson, owned a light-coloured German Shepherd mix called Sage. Jim was a huge dog lover and had other dogs, but Sage seems to have been a particular favourite. It's been reported that, when Jim was in Paris in 1971, he wired cash back for his dog minder to buy Sage some treats. Sadly, it was on this same trip that he passed away at the age of 27, leaving Sage in the care of Pamela.

Samson, Charlotte & Charlie

Actor Bradley Cooper, who celebrates his birthday today, says his dogs are his kids. His first rescue dog was Samson, a German Shorthaired Pointer, and the second, a dog called Charlotte, a Chow-Retriever mix who Bradley says he fell in love with immediately. The actor-director even cast another of his dogs, a Labradoodle called Charlie, in the hit film *A Star Is Born.* Even if they aren't in the film itself, his dogs will always get to hang out on set in his trailer and, when he is dating someone new, the actor says he will always explain, 'My dogs and I come in a package.'

6 JANUARY

All dogs

On this day in 1929, Mother Teresa travelled to Calcutta to begin her work among the poor. The Catholic missionary, who was awarded the Nobel Peace Prize in 1979 and who was canonised in 2016, was famous for her work with humans but few people knew of her love for animals. She always carried a photo of St Francis of Assisi – the patron saint of all animals – with her, saying it was because he had such a great love of animals, which was a love she shared. 'They are such simple creations of God's beauty. They give us everything without asking for anything,' she once said.

Rex

Opera singer Marian Anderson named her dog Rex after her friend
and neighbour Rex Stout. In 1955, and on this day, she became the
first African American to perform with the New York Metropolitan
Opera, singing the role of Ulrica in Giuseppe Verdi's *Un ballo
maschera*, which translates to *A Masked Ball.* Philadelphia-born
Marian performed a wide range of music from opera to spirituals,
and with the support of President Franklin D. Roosevelt and his
wife, Eleanor, gave an open-air concert on the steps of the Lincoln
Memorial on Easter Sunday in 1939.

8 JANUARY

Olive

Award-winning novelist Isabelle Allende, who once shared a dog called Olive with her second husband, makes no secret of the special place she has in her heart for the dogs in her life. Allende wrote, 'I wake up every morning in my small house in California, squeezed between my husband and two dogs and realise that love is all that truly matters.' On this day in 1981, the Chilean/American writer started a letter to her dying grandfather, which became her first novel, *The House of Spirits*. Since then, she has sold 75 million books.

9 JANUARY

Victory

Believe it or not, dogs have enjoyed a long and esteemed history in the navy – well, plenty of dogs do love water, after all. Many have come in the form of mascots, lovingly adopted by sea-going vessels. The US Navy in particular has a soft spot for the practice, with dogs such as Mike (mascot of the USS *New York*) and Randy (mascot of "H" Division on board USS *Randolph*) just two examples. One especially regarded mascot is Victory, Vicky for short, who was part of the crew of USS *Iowa* when she was first commissioned in 1943. In fact, Vicky has remained so popular that the ship now features a snack shop called Vicky's Doghouse. In this week back in 1818, the first regular transatlantic shipping service began between Liverpool and New York.

Beau

The star of the Christmas classic *It's a Wonderful Life* and the Hitchcock thriller *Rear Window,* the American actor James (Jimmy) Stewart, was so attached to Beau, his 'wilful but beloved' Golden Retriever, that he wrote an entire poem dedicated to the dog. Beau was supposed to sleep in his own bed in the corner of the bedroom Stewart shared with his wife, Gloria, but would creep over to the marital bed in the night, so the couple often woke with him lying between them, snoring happily away. 'Somehow, my touching his hair made him happier and just the feeling of him laying against me helped me sleep better,' the actor once said. Stewart also starred alongside Charlton Heston in the 1952 film *The Greatest Show on Earth*, which was premiered on this day in 1952.

11 JANUARY

Shelby

When the producers were casting for the film *A Dog's Way Home*, they were looking for that 'something special' and with former stray Shelby – the Rottweiler-German Shepherd mix who played Bella – they found it. Shelby was just one-and-a-half when she was found scavenging for food near a Tennessee animal shelter, and her carers said her tail never stopped wagging. 'It was important to have a dog that had a lot of energy and the physicality to perform the action. But I also was looking for a dog that just had that thing in her eyes,' says trainer Teresa A. Miller. The film was released on this day in 2019.

12 JANUARY

Gaspar, Melchior & Balthazar

These three lucky dogs lived in a building known as Motown Mansion since it was the home of Motown founder Berry Gordy, who established the Detroit record label (originally as Tamla Records) on this day in 1959. Gordy lived in the house through the 1960s and right up to the early 2000s and so, according to the new owner and dog lover, arts consultant Alan Brown, the house is more than a house, it's a place of musical history. Motown, which was home to artists like Stevie Wonder, Smokey Robinson, Gladys Knight, Michael Jackson and Marvin Gaye, made Gordy the one of most successful music entrepreneurs for decades.

13 JANUARY

Poker Dogs

American artist Cassius Marcellus Coolidge, who was famous for his series of 18 paintings known as *Dogs Playing Poker*, passed away on this day in 1934, aged 89. The series began in 1894 with a piece named *Poker Game*, featuring four St Bernards, and concluded in 1910. All 18 pieces feature anthropomorphised dogs seated around a card table. At the time, Coolidge himself was not widely recognised and was often ridiculed for his art. However, his pieces have subsequently been referenced in pop culture dozens of times – including in an episode of *The Simpsons* – and in 2015, his first painting in the series sold for $658,000 at auction.

14 JANUARY

Hound Dog

It's a tune known to just about every dog owner, and perhaps one that's been sung to its fair share of noisy dogs and puppies over the years too. The classic 12-bar blues song 'Hound Dog' was written by Jerry Leiber and Mike Stoller and originally recorded by Big Mama Thornton in 1952, but it's Elvis Presley's 1956 version that has struck a chord and ranked at number 19 in *Rolling Stone* magazine's 500 Greatest Songs of All Time list in 2004. Presley made headlines when he served in the US Army at the height of his fame, and he was promoted to the rank of sergeant on this day in 1960.

Poke

When American singer Lizzo ended her six-month long Cuz I Love You Too tour on this day in 2020 in Auckland, New Zealand, she and her tour crew had more to celebrate than tucking a successful tour under their belt – they also came home with a couple of rescue dogs they rehomed at the start of the tour. After visiting a local dog shelter in Madison, Wisconsin, Lizzo, who likes to promote the work of dog shelters before each concert, helped her tour driver Mike rehome a little dog they called Poke, short for Pocahontas. Another member of her crew also rehomed one of Poke's three sisters.

Stevie

'Stevie the Wonderdog' took the internet by storm in March 2020 when a video of him 'puddly dancing' went viral. The world was in the grip of a pandemic and families had been told to stay home, so Steve's natural exuberance and free spirit won him legions of fans. The hashtag #SpreadStevieJoy was shared far and wide as people learned more about Stevie's underlying condition of cerebella hypoplasia, which does not cause him any pain but does affect his motor skills and balance. And thanks to his growing popularity, Stevie had a new job – to show how his full and happy life was, living proof that all dogs with special needs deserve a loving home to thrive in too. On this day in 1978, Stevie's namesake, the actual Stevie Wonder, won an American Music Award.

17 JANUARY

Major

Born on this day in 2018, Major is a German Shepherd and holds the distinction of being the first-ever rescue dog to move into the White House, with his owners, the Bidens. Major lived first with the Biden's dog Champ, who sadly passed away at the age of 13 before a new four-legged roommate arrived in the shape of Commander, a German Shepherd puppy given to President Biden on his 79th birthday by his brother James and sister-in-law Sarah.

Mister

On this day in 1944, the Metropolitan Opera House in New York City opened its doors to host the very first jazz concert ever staged there. Performers included Louis Armstrong, Benny Goodman and a trailblazing vocalist called Eleanora Fagan, who was better known as Billie Holiday and often called Lady Day. Billie, with her distinctive vocals, ushered in a new era of singing and helped to make jazz more popular. Dogs were an important part of Billie's tumultuous life and perhaps her only source of unconditional love. Her favourite canine companion was Mister — she would knit him sweaters, cook for him and make him his favourite dinners. Mister accompanied Billie when she sang in glamorous nightclubs, in return for which she'd get the porters to bring Mister a plate of delicious home-cooked stew.

Robot

In September 1940, the Second World War was raging when an 18-year-old French boy called Marcel Ravidat and his friends were walking with his little dog, Robot. As they made their way through the woods in Montignac, the dog bolted down what appeared to be a rabbit hole by an uprooted tree – but turned out to be a passageway to an underground complex of caves. And on the walls of those caves were some 600 wall paintings, thought to be around 17,000 years old. The Lascaux Cave was opened to the public until the paintings began to deteriorate, at which point a replica site was built for tourists.

Tommy

Faithful Tommy, a seven-year-old German Shepherd, became known for his near daily visits to the church where his owner's funeral had recently taken place, sitting quietly alongside the altar during Mass. Tommy had been used to attending the church with his Italian owner, Maria Margherita Lochi, and was present at her funeral after she passed away, following after her coffin. Priest Donata Panna said, 'He waits patiently by the side of the altar and just sits there quietly. I don't have the heart to throw him out, so I leave him until the end of Mass and then I let him out.' Tommy's loyal vigil continued throughout his life until he passed away and his watch ended at last, on this day in 2014.

Crumpet

American TikTok and Instagram star and beauty influencer model Meredith Duxbury says dogs are absolutely her favourite animals, and she often posts vlogs of her face fully made up with make-up chosen by her dog, Crumpet, a honey-coloured Retriever. Meredith, who was born in 1999, celebrates her birthday today. She has made her name and garnered millions of followers on all her social media platforms by sharing her signature style of full-coverage make-up looks.

Sharp

In the 1860s and 1870s, Queen Victoria became very fond of Smooth Collies – so fond that over her long lifetime (81 years) she owned 88 in total. Her favourite of all these was the very first of them to be kept as a pet, a Collie called Sharp, acquired in 1866 soon after the death of her beloved husband, Prince Albert. The loyal dog proved the perfect companion for the grieving Queen and can be seen alongside her in various photographs. Victoria passed away on this day in 1901.

Bob The Dog

Bob is the title of an Édouard Manet oil on canvas painting believed to date to 1876. Now part of the Getty art collection, it shows a furry little dog with his hair flung in all directions, which the painter achieved by having the brush stroke go every which way. Art historians think that Bob most likely belonged to Manet's great friend, the opera singer Jean-Baptiste Faure, who was also a significant collector of his work in the late nineteenth and early twentieth centuries. It is certainly known that Manet, who was born on this day in 1832, liked to paint pet portraits for his inner circle of friends.

Foxy

Over her lifetime, the American writer and Pulitzer Prize winning author Edith Wharton had so many dogs that her house in Lenox, Massachusetts has a dog cemetery. Wharton, whose novel *The Age of Innocence* was made into a film starring Daniel Day-Lewis and Michelle Pfeiffer, was born into high society and documented the lives of the upper classes in her books. She was given her first dog, a Spitz called Foxy, at the age of four, and that was it – her love of dogs stayed with her until her death. She loved dogs so much that she based one of her books around a dog, and even wrote poetry to her canine companions.

Flush

Flush: A Biography was a blend of fiction and non-fiction written by Virginia Woolf about Elizabeth Barrett Browning's Cocker Spaniel, who was called Flush. The Bloomsbury Set novelist said she wrote it to give herself a light-hearted break following the writing of her novel *The Waves*, which was published in 1931 and which is critically regarded as her most experimental work. In *Flush*, Woolf, who was born on this day in 1882, explores the barriers that exist between a woman and an animal which are created by language and yet which can be overcome through symbolic actions. In simple terms, she wrote about the fact that your dog may not understand your every word, but will, for sure, know you love them.

26 JANUARY

Kid, Augie & Mrs Wallis Browning

American comedienne and talk-show host Ellen DeGeneres and her actress wife, Portia de Rossi, are pet parents to three rescue dogs – Kid, a Poodle/Maltese, Augie, a Beagle mix, and a Poodle called Mrs Wallis Browning, who generally goes by the simpler name of Wallis. Animal lover and advocate Ellen attributed much of her ability to survive the COVID-19 pandemic to her large pet family and all the free cuddles on offer each and every day. Ellen celebrates her birthday today and so can expect extra cuddles from her pet family members.

27 JANUARY

Donnie

Donnie the Doberman astonished his owners when he started arranging his toys in recognisable geometric patterns, including circles and triangles. He also likes to organise his toys in groupings – all the monkey toys together and face up or all the frog toys face down. Of course, nobody knows why this rescue dog does this, but Donnie was featured on a *National Geographic* programme called *Brilliant Beasts – Dog Genius*. *National Geographic* was founded on this day in 1888.

28 JANUARY

Cut & Ball

He may have gone off several of his wives, but Henry VIII remained devoted to his dogs: when he passed away, no fewer than 65 dog leads were found in his closet. Two of the king's favourite dogs were Cut and Ball. Henry was so distraught when the pair once went missing that he offered nearly 15 shillings (equivalent to around £225 today) as a reward for their return. Fond of many breeds, including Spaniels, Beagles and Greyhounds, the king's affection for his animals meant that it wasn't long before others at court followed suit. But few could rival the splendour of the dogs themselves, who wore velvet collars studded with gold or silver and carrying Henry's coat of arms and frequently embellished with pearls. Henry died on this day in 1547.

Luath

Scottish poet Robert (or Rabbie) Burns was the proud owner of a Border Collie, which he named Luath after the dog owned by Cuchullin in the epic peom 'Fingal'. And Luath's lofty literary connections don't end there. Burns immortalised his dog in his poem 'The Twa Dogs', in which he uses a conversation between two dogs – his own Border Collie and a Newfoundland called Ceasar – to present a satire on wealth and poverty. The poet is remembered each year on Burns Night, celebrated on his birthday on 25 January with the eating of haggis, neeps and tatties (turnips and potatoes), the drinking of whisky and the reciting of poems. But the first such night is actually thought to have been held on this day in 1802 by the Greenock Ayrshire Society, before they realised their mistake the following year and moved celebrations to the more familiar date that is still honoured today.

30 JANUARY

Barry

Barry – full name Barry der Menschenretter – was a Swiss
mountain rescue dog who worked in the early 1800s and who
is celebrated for saving 40 lives during his time in service.
Menschenretter is German for 'people rescuer'. Barry worked
for the Great Bernard Hospice – a monastery and hostel in the
mountains – and ever since his time, there has always been a dog
there named Barry after him. His story has featured in numerous
books and there is even a monument to him in the Cimetière
des Chiens near Paris. Equally inspired by Barry's story, Disney
released a two-part telefilm called *Barry, of the Great St. Bernard*
on this day in 1977.

31 JANUARY

'The Pup'

On this day in 1862, the American telescope-maker and astronomer
Alvan Graham Clark first observed what looked like a faint
companion to the Dog Star, known as Sirius. Now called Sirius B –
and affectionately named 'the Pup' – the star is described as one of
the most massive white dwarfs, with a mass that is almost as big (98
per cent) as our own sun. Sirius itself has a mass two times that of
the Sun and a diameter of 2.4 million km (1.5 million miles), and at
8.6 light years away is one of the nearest known stars to the Earth.

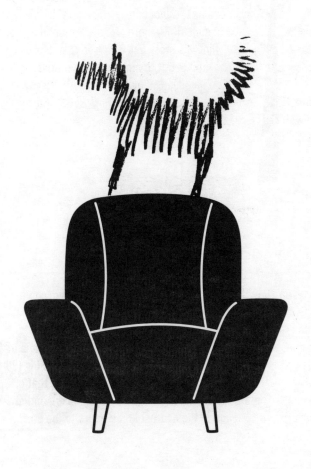

FEBRUARY

1 FEBRUARY

Bobi

Bobi, a Portuguese dog, was crowned the world's oldest dog ever on this day in 2023 – aged 30 years and 266 days. Bobi currently holds two records – he is both the oldest living dog, and the oldest dog ever! Bobi lives in Conqueiros, a small village in Portugal, with his owner Leonel Costa. Bobi's owners attribute his longevity to the fact that he is free to wander across acres of forest and farmland, and to love and affection from them.

2 FEBRUARY

Balto

Balto is remembered as the plucky, young and inexperienced sled dog whose tenacity and big heart helped get a life-saving serum to the population of Nome in Alaska in 1925. Doctors had started to see symptoms of the deadly infection diphtheria in the town, but the nearest serum was 800 km (500 miles) away and the brutal winter made travel impossible. The sole route was a 1,050-km (650-mile) freight route which normally took a month to travel. The town organised a dog sled relay to get the serum and young Balto was paired with an older, more experienced dog, called Togo. The duo, both Siberian Huskies, ran the last leg of the relay and charged into the town just before dawn on 2 February.

3 FEBRUARY

Raleigh

The American artist Norman Rockwell liked to paint real people and real animals, and went to a lot of trouble to capture the spirit of the dog he was painting. So it's perhaps not surprising that Norman, born on this day in 1894, had a dog of his own: a Collie known as Raleigh. Rockwell's paintings were generally joyous and captured a certain sweetness and nostalgia in his subjects, and he was known for asking his neighbours – and their pets – to pose for him, to enable him to capture not just the likeness but also the spirit of a real-life model. Raleigh Rockwell was, of course, used as just such a model by his artistic owner, including in a 1929 painting called *Boy with Two Dogs*.

Beast

Facebook CEO and co-founder Mark Zuckerberg and his wife, Priscilla Chan, are dog parents to an extra woolly Puli (a type of Hungarian sheepdog) called Beast, who looks like a giant mop! Of course, Beast has his own Facebook page, as do some 7 per cent of family dogs, whose owners have set up pages for them. When the couple's toddler daughter hit the milestone of her first word, Mark Zuckerman told Facebook users, 'She loves Beast, and of course her first word was "dog"'. Facebook itself, which was founded on this day in 2004, has a reported 2.963 billion users across the world.

Mutt

Mutt starred in the first comedy film ever made by Charlie Chaplin in his own studios. The film was called *A Dog's Life* and tells the story of Scraps, a dog that belongs to a man (played by Chaplin) who is down on his luck and trying to find a place for himself in society. It was one of the few films where Charlie abandoned his distinctive trademark walking cane but perhaps only because he had Scraps on a leash to make up for it. The First World War was already raging when Chaplin opened his studio and so the film was finished in a rush to allow the comedian to 'do his bit' by touring the nation selling Liberty Bonds in support of the war effort. And on this day the following year (1919), the actor launched United Artists with fellow actors Mary Pickford, Douglas Fairbanks and D.W. Griffith.

Toby

American writer John Steinbeck's classic book *Of Mice and Men* – which tells the story of George and Lennie, a couple of migrant ranch workers in the Great Depression – almost never saw the light of day thanks to the antics of the author's puppy, an Irish Setter called Toby. The first draft of the book, which was first published on this day in 1937, was lying around the house when the puppy decided to shred most of it. The writer came home to find his work reduced to a pile of paper confetti and had no choice but to tidy up, sit down and write it all again.

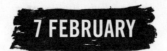

7 FEBRUARY

Cap

Did you know it was a dog that led nursing legend Florence Nightingale to find her calling? The story goes that when she was just 17, Florence had helped to heal a local shepherd's dog, who was called Cap and who had a wounded back leg. Florence nursed Cap back to health using hot compresses. The following night – 7 February 1837 – Florence had a prophetic vision in which she claims she heard the voice of God telling her it was her purpose to heal people. She started nursing in the Crimean War and soon became known as the Lady with the Lamp, thanks to her habit of checking on the wounded by walking the wards carrying an oil lamp. She was the first woman to ever receive the British Order of Merit.

Daisy

Daisy was the white Labrador who flew with a cargo of rescue dogs from California to Canada in a bid to save the dogs who were at risk from wildfires and who needed new homes. She was accompanied by her owner, the actor Kevin Costner, who was the star of *Dances with Wolves,* which was released on this day in 1991. A lifelong dog lover, Kevin went on to voice a dog called Enzo in the 2019 film *The Art Of Racing.*

Weston

Although he was more of a 'cat man', George Harrison did have a little Yorkshire Terrier called Weston, who was named after John Lennon, Weston being John's middle name. George was, of course, the lead guitarist of the Beatles, who performed for the first time on *The Ed Sullivan* show on this day in 1964, drawing a record-breaking audience of 73 million viewers. The Fab Four, who went on to sell a certified 183 million albums worldwide, remain the top-selling artists of all time.

10 FEBRUARY

Yogi

A newspaper reporter once asked the singer-songwriter Roberta Flack about her New Year's resolutions for her pets, including her eight (at the time) rescue dogs. She bounced straight back with her answer, saying she'd like to not have to beg her Shiba Inu dog, Yogi, to eat from his bowl. 'He likes to be begged to eat... given one bite at a time by hand,' she explained. Roberta, who was born on this day in 1937, tweeted on National Love Your Pet Day, 'So much love for my rescued animal friends.' And it turns out those friends include donkeys, horses, chickens and flamingos, as well as dogs!

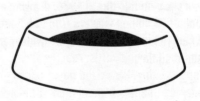

Gompo

On this day in 1990, Nelson Mandela, who was to become the first Black leader of South Africa, was released from prison after 27 years, 18 of which he served in a maximum-security prison on Robben Island. After his release, Mandela helped negotiate the end of apartheid and became the first democratically elected president of South Africa. Before his arrest and imprisonment, Nelson had a dog called Gompo, a Rhodesian Ridgeback who was often photographed with him at the home which has now been turned into a museum.

Gromit

Happy Birthday today to one of the most loved fictional dogs ever created – Gromit, of animated Wallace & Gromit fame. We know today is the little dog's birthday because, in the *The Wrong Trousers,* we see him circling the date on the calendar. According to the show's Fandom page, the puzzle-loving Gromit, who is clearly the brains of the duo, graduated from Dogwarts University with a double first in Engineering for Dogs. We also learn that Gromit enjoys knitting, playing cards, reading the newspaper, building things and cooking. His prized possessions include an alarm clock, bone, brush and a framed photo of himself with Wallace, of whom he is genuinely very fond.

13 FEBRUARY

Tara

In the film *Oliver Twist*, the character Bill Sikes – owner of English Bulldog, Bull's-eye – was something of an unsavoury character. But in real life, the late English actor Oliver Reed, who played the role of Sikes in the popular film adaptation of the story, loved and spoiled Tara, the Great Dane he took home from Battersea. In public, he may have been known for his tough performances and something of a hellraiser lifestyle, but when it came to his new dog it seems he was a big softie. He fell in love with the dog and the duo soon became inseparable. Oliver was born on this day in 1938.

14 FEBRUARY

Lucho & George

It's the day of love and, for lots of us, that means love for our dogs! For Hollywood star Ryan Gosling and his wife, Eva Mendes, all that love gets poured into Lucho, the Doberman puppy they rehomed in 2019. Before that, it was a dog called George who held Ryan's heart, the actor telling a talk show that George was always more human than dog. 'He was always a good friend to me – there was something about George where I think he thought being a dog was a bit beneath him. He wouldn't do tricks, and if you wanted him to sit, you had to convince him it was in his best interest... ' Now that's dog love talking!

15 FEBRUARY

Clifford

Clifford the Big Red Dog is the name of a series of children's books written by American illustrator Norman Bridwell, who named the giant, red-furred dog after his wife's imaginary childhood friend. Born on this day in 1928, Norman was working at Harper & Row when an editor there offhandedly suggested he could turn one of his drawings of a girl and a horse-sized Bloodhound into a story. Norman went on to turn that first drawing into a series of 80 books and a 65-episode TV adaptation. Clifford even visited the White House and took part in the 2007 Easter Egg Roll with the then First Lady, Laura Bush, and a gang of little kids.

16 FEBRUARY

Abuwtiyuw

A dog in the royal household of an unknown pharaoh, Abuwtiyuw is one of the first domesticated dogs in history whose name is known. Dogs were an important symbolic part of ancient Egyptian culture, and when the British archaeologist Howard Carter opened up the tomb of pharaoh Tutankhamun on this day in 1923, he found a striking statue of a dog. Carter himself was the son of an artist father who painted mainly dogs for rich local clients, and it was through his dad that he met an Egyptologist who arranged for the then 17-year-old to travel to Egypt to help record the artwork being uncovered in the tombs and temples there.

Meg

In the first-ever series of the popular BBC2 TV show *One Man and His Dog,* which centred on the agility and obedience of working sheepdogs, the singles trophy went to Meg and her owner, David Sheehan. The first show aired on this day in 1976 and, while the regular series ended in 1990, it would return with Christmas Specials each year and eventually became a special edition of *Countryfile.* The term 'sheepdog' describes any breed that has been developed to herd sheep but is used most often to describe a Border Collie.

18 FEBRUARY

I Know, You Know & Don't Know

A little different from Rover or Fido, these were the names that the American writer, Mark Twain, gave his three beloved Collie dogs. Twain, who published *The Adventures of Huckleberry Finn* on this day in 1885, was a huge dog lover and is reported to have once said, 'The more I learn about people, the more I like my dog!' Huckleberry Finn tells the story of a barely literate teenage boy who fakes his own death to escape his abusive father. He meets a runaway called Jim and the two set off on a raft journey down the Mississippi River.

19 FEBRUARY

Doogal

Doogal is the dog in the 1960s children's television show *The Magic Roundabout*. A stout and drop-eared Skye Terrier, Doogal is a happy-go-lucky chap who is the main protagonist in the show and whose friends include Zebedee, a talking jack-in-the-box, a cow called Dylan (named after Bob Dylan) and a hippy rabbit called Flappy. In 2005, the characters reappeared in *The Magic Roundabout: The Movie.* Robbie Williams voiced Doogal and the British 'hard man' actor, Ray Winstone, who celebrates his birthday today, voiced Soldier Sam.

20 FEBRUARY

Susan

Susan was the Pembroke Corgi given to Her Majesty Queen Elizabeth II by her father for her 18th birthday, making her the first in a long line of Corgis so beloved by the Queen. In fact, all but two of her Corgis were descended from Susan, who could do no wrong in the eyes of her mistress. The young princess was so enamoured of her dog that she even took her on her honeymoon when she married her husband of 73 years, Prince Philip. Susan, whose registered name was Hickathrift Pippa, was born on this day in 1944.

21 FEBRUARY

Trouve

Trouve, which means 'find' in French, was the name of the rescue Skye Terrier who was the childhood pet of the inventor of the telephone, Alexander Graham Bell. Bell was the son of a father and grandfather who had both devoted their lives to helping the deaf learn to speak, and early in his career he had chosen the same path. Part of his research involved an attempt to teach little Trouve to speak. And he was successful in teaching the little Terrier to make vowel sounds, leading to the dog becoming famous in his own right, being dubbed 'The Talking Dog' by the press. (In truth, of course, Trouve only 'spoke' on command.) Today marks the anniversary of the issue of what is believed to be the world's first telephone directory in New Haven, Connecticut.

Douglas, Lucy & Oliver

Actor Drew Barrymore, who shot to fame as a child playing the role of Gertie in the Stephen Spielberg film *E.T. the Extra-Terrestrial*, is a big supporter of rehoming dogs and has three rescue pets, including a Labrador mix called Douglas. Lucy is a Golden Retriever and Oliver is a German Shepherd mix. Drew, who was born on this day in 1975, admits her beloved pets sleep on her bed and says it has never crossed her mind to do anything but rescue.

23 FEBRUARY

Finley

Lots of dogs like a tennis ball – or two – but Finley the Golden Retriever holds the new Guinness World Record for having 'the most tennis balls held in the mouth by a dog' after holding six balls in his mouth on this day in 2020. Finley, who lives in New York, loves swimming, and playing fetch and chase. Finley's obsession with tennis balls started as a puppy and he soon became a 'ball hoarder' according to his owner, Erin. The furry tennis balls are said to encourage the breed's natural drive to retrieve, so it's no surprise that Finley is such a fan.

24 FEBRUARY

Bodie

Puppy Bodie is an Australian Shepherd mix who belongs to actor Brianne Howey, who plays mum Georgia in the Netflix hit *Ginny & Georgia*. When Brianne and her husband, Matt Ziering, tied the knot in June 2021, Bodie was present to witness the couple making their vows. In interviews, Brianne has admitted she might be 'overly obsessed' with her gorgeous dog, who joined the family in 2020. 'He was the biggest heart-opener,' she has said. 'I can be so cranky and in the worst mood or just feeling so down and in my head and having a hard time getting out of whatever rut, and I just go hang out with my Bodie... and it's the best!' *Ginny & Georgia* premiered on this day in 2021.

25 FEBRUARY

Lulu

Dog is the title of a 2022 road-trip comedy starring Channing Tatum, who has to race down the Pacific Coast with a military dog called Lulu in a madcap bid to get her to her handler's funeral on time. Lulu is a Belgian Malinois who was played by three different dogs and her performance got the thumbs up from the US military, which, according to the Department of Defense, employs about 1,600 dogs, serving in every branch and skilled in everything from search and rescue to drug and explosive detection. Channing, who co-directed the film, made his own screen debut in *Coach Carter*, which was released on this day in 2005.

Uggie

When the French-made film *The Artist* was first shown at Cannes Film Festival in 2011, it was the four-legged star, a Jack Russell called Uggie, who stole our hearts. The comedy-drama was made in the style of an old black-and-white silent Hollywood film and went on to win five Oscars the following year, including Best Picture. But, of course, it's the talented Uggie we all remember best. Uggie was so loved that he even went on stage on this day in 2012 with his co-stars, Jean Dujardin and Bérénice Bejo, to accept one of those Oscars, presented at the 84th Academy Awards.

Pal

For her 60th birthday, actor Elizabeth Taylor became the owner of a Collie puppy, which was a great-grandpuppy (seven generations back) of Pal, the dog who played the original Lassie in the *Lassie* films. As a teen, Elizabeth had played Priscilla, the daughter of the Duke of Rudling, in the very first Lassie film, called *Lassie Come Home*. She appeared again with Pal three years later in *Courage of Lassie*. When the actor ended her marriage to construction worker Larry Fortensky, who had been her eighth husband, the couple fought over who would have the dog, with Elizabeth successfully gaining custody.

28 FEBRUARY

Ranger

M*A*S*H fans may remember seeing a glimpse of Radar's dog, Ranger, when an episode of the US hit TV show features a home movie showing us Radar's life before he was sent to a Mobile Army Surgical Hospital (MASH) in the Korean War. The doctors stationed there do everything they can to keep people alive, using humour to face the gruesome realities of the war and its casualties. Hapless Walter 'Radar' O'Reilly, who was shown to be very fond of animals, was played by the animal-loving actor Gary Burghoff. The character was given his nickname because of his uncanny ability to show up before he was called for and because he could sense incoming helicopters before anyone else in camp. The final episode of *M*A*S*H* aired on this day in 1983 and was watched by a record-holding 106 million viewers.

Chow Puppy

This leap year bonus entry tells the story of Augusta Savage, an American sculptor who was at the heart of the Harlem Renaissance art movement and who campaigned for equal rights for African Americans in the arts. Born on this day in 1892, the daughter of a Methodist minister, Augusta would fashion small figures, including dogs, out of natural red clay, but her father was vehemently opposed to her early interest in art, which he believed to be a sinful practice. Augusta, who had a Chow puppy, once said, 'I was a leap year baby, and it seems to me I've been leaping ever since.'

MARCH

1 MARCH

Romeo

An English Bull Terrier from Buxton made his stage debut on this day in 2019 playing Bull's-eye, the dog that belonged to baddie Bill Sykes in a local production of the Charles Dickens' classic *Oliver Twist*. Romeo, who was aged two-and-a-half at the time and who has a brown patch around one eye just like the original dog that played the part, has a 91-cm (36-inch) chest and weighs over 32 kg (5 stone). Romeo was described as 'loveable' in local press previews of the show. Owner Nick, who rescues Bull Terriers, said of him, 'He's just a big baby who loves cuddles.'

2 MARCH

Zeppelin

Jack Russell Terrier-Schnauzer Zeppelin doesn't know the meaning of the word 'starstruck'. His owner is the American *Fifty Shades of Grey* actor Dakota Johnson, who is the daughter of actors Don Johnson and Melanie Griffiths. If that weren't enough, her partner is Coldplay frontman Chris Martin, who celebrates his birthday today. Jet-setting Dakota doesn't go anywhere without Zeppelin, who she rehomed from a rescue, so it's fair to say he's become pretty used to the high life.

Winnie

Winnie is the family pet of Clementine, daughter of actor Cybil Shepherd, and it seems it's a case of like mother, like daughter because Cybil is also a dog lover and currently has three dogs of her own. Winnie, a Golden Retriever mix, is a rescue who joined Clementine's family in 2021. The little dog hit the headlines when a woman pretending to be an approved dog minder made off with her but, happily, she was returned home safely after Clementine appealed for help in finding her via Instagram. Today marks the first airing of the sitcom *Moonlighting* in which Cybil starred opposite a wisecracking detective played by Bruce Willis in a show that shot them both to international fame.

4 MARCH

Fala

On this day in 1933, President Franklin D. Roosevelt was inaugurated as the 32nd President of the United States. He was to lead the country out of the Great Depression and to victory in the Second World War. One of many White House occupants (before and after his presidency) to move in with a four-legged companion, Roosevelt had a little Scottish Terrier called Fala. Given to the President by a cousin, Fala would entertain the media with his clever tricks and became so famous he is now remembered with his own Wikipedia page. The little dog outlived his owner by seven years but was eventually buried near him.

5 MARCH

Buck, Jess & Ace

Black Labrador Buck makes regular appearances on his owner Niki Taylor's Instagram, often when the duo have just finished their daily morning jog. The American supermodel and TV host, who was the youngest model ever to sign a six-figure deal at the age of just 14, celebrates her birthday today with a house full of rescue dogs and says, 'Life is so short, it's too much to take things too seriously. That's one of the things I love so much about animals. They don't take anything too seriously and are always happy to see you.'

6 MARCH

Patch

Patch was the late television presenter John Noake's first *Blue Peter* dog and arrived in 1965. He was one of Petra's puppies (*see* 16 October). Yorkshireman John, who was born John Bottomley in Halifax on this day in 1934, was the show's longest-serving presenter with a tenure that lasted 12 years, 6 months. He had originally trained as an actor and made his own stage debut playing a dog and a clown in a summer show with the comedian Cyril Fletcher. John also took care of Shep, who came after Patch, and so a whole generation grew up hearing John's catchphrase: 'Get down, Shep!'

7 MARCH

Merlin

They may be the stars of the show, but they are occasionally upstaged by the appearance of a particularly handsome co-star called Merlin. If you haven't guessed already, we're talking about Wiltshire-based *Gogglebox* favourites Giles Wood and Mary Killen, who have been on the hit Channel 4 show since 2015. Merlin is a Tibetan Spaniel, a breed said to have been favoured as companions by Tibetan monks living in monasteries. Gogglebox was first screened on this day in 2013.

8 MARCH

Taylor-Douglas

On 8 March 1817, the now world-famous New York Stock Exchange was created. It became one of the world's largest marketplaces for securities and other exchange-related investments and was also the backdrop for the 1987 film *Wall Street,* which tells the story of Bud Fox, played by Charlie Sheen, as the young stockbroker who becomes entangled with the wealthy and unscrupulous corporate raiser Gordon Gekko, played by Michael Douglas. Douglas, along with his wife, Catherine Zeta-Jones, is the owner of a rescue Maltipoo named Taylor-Douglas.

9 MARCH

Fortuné

Having married on this day in 1796 for love and passion rather than political gain, Napoleon Bonaparte was deeply unimpressed on his wedding night when he eagerly pulled back the bed covers only to find his new wife's little Pug Fortuné lying alongside her mistress. And when he tried to oust the little dog, he was shown just whose bed it was by the cross Pug. Napoleon knew when he was beat and, from that moment, the three slept together each night.

10 MARCH

Charlotte 'Charlie' Nilla Fisher

In her song 'The More Boys I Meet', *American Idol* winner Carrie Underwood sings about how, with the more boys she meets, the more she loves her dog over them. Carrie is proud owner of rescue dog Charlie, who joined the family in early 2023. And dog lover Carrie, who won the fourth season of *American Idol* in 2005, celebrates her birthday today. Describing Charlie as 'the right pup' for her family, she introduced fans to the dog via Instagram, explaining that she met the shelter puppy while on tour.

11 MARCH

Timber Doodle

Timber Doodle was the Havana Spaniel taken everywhere by the writer Charles Dickens after acquiring him on a trip to America. Although best known for his novels such as *Oliver Twist, A Tale of Two Cities* and *A Christmas Carol,* Dickens started life as a journalist. In 1834, he worked as a parliamentary reporter for the *Morning Chronicle,* a national daily newspaper, and by 1846, he was publishing his own newspaper, called the *Daily News.* On this day in 1702, the *Daily Courant,* England's first national daily newspaper, was published for the first time.

12 MARCH

Potchky

The iconic American novelist Jack Kerouac, whose bestselling book *On The Road* defined the newly emerging Beat generation, was born on this day in 1922. Jack, who wrote the manuscript at breakneck speed in just 20 days, once described how he created a scroll using tracing paper cut to fit the width of his typewriter. By the end of the book, the scroll was 37 m (120 feet) long but, unfortunately, the end was missing because Potchky, a Cocker Spaniel owned by the writer's friend, Lucien Carr, had nibbled it. Or so the story goes... in fact there were those who claimed Kerouac himself had torn the last lines from the scroll because he couldn't settle on an ending he liked. What is true is that 50 years after it was created, the scroll was sold at auction for a staggering $2.43 million.

13 MARCH

Arnie

Kaya Scodelario, who celebrates her birthday today, is owner of
Arnie, who has his own Twitter account in which he describes
himself as the 'luckiest dog on earth'. Sharing her joy at sharing
her life with her dog, Kaya wrote on her Instagram pages, 'Now,
I know Arnie's "just a dog" but he really is so much more to me.'
Kaya, whose mother is Brazilian, adopted her mother's surname
and spoke Portuguese at home. She shot to fame at the age of 14
playing Effy Stonem in the E4 teen drama *Skins* and, in 2010, she
played Cathy in Andrea Arnold's adaptation of *Wuthering Heights*.
As a newcomer to the *Pirates of the Caribbean* franchise, she was
told off on set by the dog handler when she went to pet the dog.
Apparently the trainer told her, 'Excuse me, please don't disrupt
the actor, he's working!'

Bruno & Bella

On this day in 1973, pop superstars ABBA released 'Ring Ring', their first Swedish No. 1 hit and their debut release in the UK. The track was originally credited to Björn & Benny, Agnetha & Anni-Frid and was selected as Sweden's 1973 Eurovision Song Contest entry, finishing third. A year later, under the name ABBA, the group won the same competition with their international breakthrough song 'Waterloo'. Agnetha, who disappeared from the limelight when the band broke up in 1982, is a lifelong dog lover and is currently the proud owner of dogs Bruno and Bella.

Popeye

Desperate Housewives actor Eva Longoria sent baby blankets home from the hospital when she had her son Santiago so that her beloved dog, Popeye, would get used to the new arrival's smell. Eva, who celebrates her birthday today, starred in the 2018 romantic comedy *Dog Days,* which follows the intertwining lives of various dogs and their owners around Los Angeles. Eva plays a character called Grace who, along with husband Kurt, played by comedian Rob Corddry, is in the throes of adopting a daughter and struggling with the preparations for her arrival. Rob has no dogs but does have a hedgehog tattoo!

16 MARCH

Rin Tin Tin

In the late 1920s, the Academy of Motion Picture Arts and Sciences established its award ceremony for the movie business — now, of course, known as the Oscars. But at the very first awards show in 1929, legend has it that the coveted Best Actor prize almost went to a particularly handsome leading man: German Shepherd Rin Tin Tin. Born in France but rehomed by an American soldier who trained him for movie work, Rin Tin Tin (or Rinty as his owner nicknamed him) was huge box-office star in his day, appearing in nearly 30 Hollywood films. The Hollywood story goes that the canine star actually received the most votes in the Best Actor category and so should by rights have won, only for the Academy to step in and re-run the vote with Rin Tin Tin excluded. Whether or not the story is true has been the subject of debate in movie circles for many a year, but Rin Tin Tin would win the vote of dog owners every time. The Academy Awards were first referred to in print as the Oscars on this day in 1934, by American writer and Hollywood gossip columnist Sidney Skolsky.

Black Dog

English children's book illustrator Kate Greenaway, who was born on this day in 1846, often depicted dogs and puppies in her work. After studying at the Slade School of Art, Kate spent her career designing for the then burgeoning holiday card market, producing Christmas and Valentine cards. Her father was an engraver who was commissioned to produce the engraved illustrations for an edition of Charles Dickens' *The Pickwick Papers* and her mother was a dressmaker. The Kate Greenaway Medal, established in 1955, is still awarded to illustrators of children's books. The 2013 winner was Levi Pinfold, whose stunning picture book was called *Black Dog*.

Redford

Redford is a Pug-Terrier cross who belongs to actor Lily Collins (daughter of the singer-songwriter Phil) and her filmmaker husband, Charlie McDowell. The couple rehomed Redford in 2019, which means the little dog has travelled the world with the *Emily in Paris* Netflix star. The delighted owners introduced the little one via their Instagram accounts with Lily, who celebrates her birthday today, writing, 'It was love at first sight.' She added, 'Never not napping.' To which husband Charlie quipped, 'Never not napping except for when he's chewing my fingers and toes off for hours on end.'

19 MARCH

Pip

Pip is the dog of Hollywood actor Glenn Close, who celebrates her birthday today. The Havanese, formally known as Sir Pippen of Beanfield, is in danger of eclipsing his owner's fame, as he's become an Instagram star. Pip likes to document both his jet-setting travels and, of course, his many naps – his captions are often hilarious. His social media presence is said to strike the perfect balance between humble bragging and giving his followers an insight into the exhausting business of being famous. He's even tried scene stealing in the film *The Wife*, which starred his owner, but the director got wind of his antics and cut him.

20 MARCH

Zero

In the classic 1941 film *High Sierra*, the lead character is a fugitive played by Humphrey Bogart who grows very attached to a small stray dog named Pard. The dog plays a critical role in the plot and in the end is rehomed by the fugitive. When the title credits roll, we learn the dog's name in real life was Zero, owned by none other than Bogart himself. 'Bogie', as he was known, was a huge dog lover and had dogs his whole life. The actor went on to win a Best Actor Oscar at the 24th Academy Awards on this day in 1952 for his role as Charlie Allnut in *The African Queen*.

Rowlf

'Rowlf the Dog' is a Muppet character created and originally performed by Jim Henson. Known best as the resident pianist on the sketch comedy television series *The Muppet Show*, Rowlf is a scruffy brown dog of indeterminate breed with a rounded black nose and long floppy ears. Rowlf was, in fact, the first Muppet built by Don Sahlin and, unlike most of the early Muppets, he was designed as a live-hand Muppet and also one of the first non-abstract characters because he was very clearly a big dog! According to Henson's original show notes, other names considered for Rowlf were Barkley, Woffington, Barksville, Barkus, Howlington, Waggington and Beowulf. The film *Muppets Most Wanted* was released on this day in 2014.

22 MARCH

Hank, Lou, Minnie Pearl & Major

On screen she was dog mum to a Chihuahua called Bruiser Woods – real name Moonie – who was the four-legged star of the box-office hits *Legally Blonde 1 & 2*, but in real life, actor Reese Witherspoon has four of her own dogs. In fact, the *Big Little Lies* star and producer makes no secret of her love of dogs because she's always sharing photos of her dog family on her social media. Reese likes to name her dogs after other celebrities – Hank, for example, is named after country star Hank Williams. The New Orleans native, who also has three children, was born on this day in 1976.

23 MARCH

Roscoe

National Puppy Day which takes place on 23 March every year celebrates the sheer joy of puppies and the unconditional love and affection they bring into our lives. Of course, as well as spoiling the puppy (young or old) in your life, it is the best excuse ever for flooding your social media with adorable dog pics – and what loved-up dog owner can resist that? One of our favourite posts in 2023 was from racing driver Alex Bowman, who posted a photo of his (older) dogs Roscoe, a rescued Beagle mix, and Finn, a charcoal Labrador Retriever, with the joyous caption, 'Young at heart!'

Radley, Roman & Chaplain

Rescue advocate and actor Jessica Chastain says she has rehomed every dog she's ever had – and suggests that the dogs have gone on to help shape her outlook on life. At the moment, Jessica, who celebrates her birthday today, looks after Radley, a Corgi-Spaniel mix; Roman, a Chihuahua mix; and Chaplain, a three-legged mixed breed who, she says, is always trying to get on set when she's filming. 'The greatest lesson I have ever learned from rescue animals is that they don't feel sorry for themselves,' she once said.

25 MARCH

Kissy

Sex and The City star Sarah Jessica Parker shares a little Jack Russell dog called Kissy with husband Matthew Broderick. One of Kissy's best friends is Wacha, who belongs to Sarah's friend, the TV presenter Andy Cohen. The dogs go to the same New York pet club and also staycation together when their respective owners have to be away for work.

26 MARCH

Yorkie & Morkie

Aerosmith frontman Steve Tyler has two dogs – a Maltese and a Yorkie mix – hence the dogs' affectionate names. The former *American Idol* judge says, 'Dogs have a lot of love to give,' and makes no secret of his own love of our four-legged pals. 'The Reason A Dog' is a track on the band's *Done with Mirrors* album and offers a pearl of wisdom, explaining that dogs are as popular as they are because, instead of wagging their tongue, they simply wag their tails... Steve celebrates his birthday today.

27 MARCH

Pickles

Pickles was considered a national hero when he found one of football's most treasured possessions, the World Cup trophy, which had been stolen in 1966. The black-and-white Collie, who had never so much as kicked a ball himself, was walking with owner David Corbett in south London when he started playing with a package on the ground. England had been tipped to win the World Cup that year – which they did, defeating West German by 4 goals to 2 – and the trophy had gone on display in Westminster. But before the exhibit could open to the public, the gold Jules Rimet Trophy was stolen. Pickles was rewarded with £5,000 and a silver medal, and he and his owner were invited to celebrate England's momentous win with the national football team.

28 MARCH

Buckeye & Vanadis

Actor Vince Vaughn, the star of *Old School, Wedding Crashers, The Lost World: Jurassic Park* and *Dodgeball: A True Underdog Story*, has a dog called Buckeye. Vince, who was born in Minneapolis, Minnesota in 1970, celebrates his birthday today and bucks a family trend with his choice of name for his dog. When he was growing up, his mum insisted everyone, even the family pets, should have the initials VV. With sisters named Valerie and Victoria, Vince says his mum would resort to the dictionary to find 'V' names for their pets and so at one time they had a Chihuahua called Vanadis. 'To go out in the suburbs with the name Vince Vaughn and be calling for Vanadis Vaughn to come home is not exactly the coolest thing you could be doing,' he once said.

Pudsey

The first-ever animal winner of the TV show *Britain's Got Talent*, superstar dog Pudsey went on to become a household name, meeting royalty and even starring in the Royal Variety Performance at the Royal Albert Hall in London on 19 November 2012. After the show, Pudsey and his owner, Ashley, met the late Queen. Earlier that same year, the double act had won the sixth series of the talent show. Pudsey, a Border Collie, Bichon Frisé and Chinese Crested Powderpuff cross, wowed the judges, week after week, with his incredible performances. The Royal Albert Hall was opened on this day in 1871 by another royal dog lover, Queen Victoria, who was Battersea's first-ever patron.

Major

This Black Labrador-Retriever mix belongs to *Pretty Woman* and *Mystic Pizza* star Julia Roberts. Julia is clearly a dog lover because, when she married cameraman Danny Moder back in 2004, her wedding gift from her new husband was also a Black Lab, who she called Louie. Julia also starred more recently as the Wicked Queen in *Mirror Mirror*, which was a re-imagining of the classic fairytale *Snow White* and was released on this day in 2012.

31 MARCH

Diamond

A Pomeranian called Diamond – who was Sir Isaac Newton's favourite dog – might have changed the course of science and history after knocking over a candle and setting light to 25 years' worth of scribbled notes in Newton's lab. Luckily, the notes – which dated back to the 1680s – survived, though scorched, and were eventually sold at auction in December 2020 for £380,000. Newton, of course, formulated gravitational theory after questioning why an apple fell downwards and not, say, sideways or up. He died on this day in 1727.

APRIL

Lucky Dolittle

Dr Dolittle is the main character in a series of children's books written by Hugh Lofting, who published *The Story of Doctor Dolittle*, the first book in the series, in 1920. John Dolittle lives in the fictional town of Puddleby-on-the-Marsh in England and has very few human friends but, thanks to his unique gift, many animal companions. In the books, young John was taught the language of animals by his parrot, Polynesia, but in the 1998 film version, she's replaced by a dog called Lucky. Eddie Murphy, who plays Dr Dolittle in the film franchise, celebrates his birthday today.

Savannah

Savannah is believed to be the first and the only dog to have ever walked around the world, clocking up a staggering 40,230km (25,000 miles) with owner Tom Turchich, who spent 7 years walking through 38 countries, crossing every single continent except Australia (which was effectively closed due to the COVID-19 pandemic). Tom, who left his New Jersey home to start his walk on this day in 2015, found Savannah in Austin, Texas, where she had been abandoned. He walked a monumental 45,060km (28,000 miles) in total and says Savannah became both his company and his security because he could sleep at night knowing she was listening out for intruders.

Tiny

When the 1950s singing superstar and animal activist Doris Day was recovering from a car accident, her mother gave her a little dog called Tiny to cheer her up, thus beginning a long love affair with dogs. The accident, which ended the young Doris's dancing career, was actually the catalyst for the then 15-year-old to start singing instead. Known affectionately by her friends as 'the dog catcher of Beverly Hills' as an adult, Doris, who was born on this day in 1922, would often find unwanted dogs left on her doorstep and so she would take them to the dwellings of fellow stars and lobby for them to be rehomed. As one anonymous star commented, 'We all had at least one of those "Doris Day" animals!'

4 APRIL

Kubrick & Sturges

Happy Birthday to animal-lover film actor Robert Downey Jr., who remembered how his filmmaker father liked to name the family's dogs after film directors, which meant they had Kubrick (after Stanley) and Sturges (after Preston). Robert remembers being especially close to Sturges, a Yorkshire terrier. Today, the actor and his wife, Susan, live with an entourage of rescue animals at their home in Malibu. Robert also played Dr Doolittle in a 2020 version of the film and says the pets he lives with in real life helped him connect to the eccentric character of someone who can talk to animals.

5 APRIL

Sui

The late adventurer Steve Irwin loved his dog, Sui, so much he named his daughter, Bindi, after him – Sue is her middle name! The world famous zookeeper and conservationist often had Sui, a Staffordshire Bull Terrier, with him on his wild adventures and the two were great friends. The first series of Steve's TV show, *The Crocodile Hunter*, aired on this day in 1997. Steve and his wife, Terri, established large private wildlife refuges across Australia and founded the international organisation Wildlife Warriors to promote wildlife conservation, education and research.

6 APRIL

Reese

In 2016, Chloe Kim, then just 17, became the first American woman to win a gold medal in snowboarding at the Winter Youth Olympic Games, earning the highest snowboarding score in Youth Olympic Games history. Chloe went on to win gold again in 2022. When she's not training, Chloe hangs out with her dog, Reese, who is a miniature Australian Shepherd dog. The Olympian and her dog love to trek together and Chloe says time with Reese makes the magical moments in her life. She told one interviewer, 'Those moments when we're out and about exploring together — those are the moments I cherish so much.' The first modern Olympic Games opened in Athens on this day in 1896.

7 APRIL

Goofy

Goofy is the much-loved animated cartoon dog created by Walt Disney Studios. He is a very tall, anthropomorphic dog who typically wears a turtleneck and vest with pants, shoes, white gloves and a crumpled fedora hat. Goofy is a close friend of Mickey Mouse and Donald Duck. He has a son called Max Goofy and, in the film *A Goofy Movie,* which was released on this day in 1995, he drags his son on a cross-country trip to distract him from falling in love with a girl in school.

8 APRIL

Mookie & Sam

Actor Kyle MacLachlan, who played mystery-solving Dale 'Damn Fine Cup of Coffee' Cooper in the brilliantly twisted cult classic TV show *Twin Peaks*, which aired its first episode on this day in 1990, went on to make an even more subversive show when he created a YouTube series starring his own dogs, Mookie and Sam. Following the show's titular heroes as they take on New York City, a trip to the seaside and even a Halloween special, Mookie and Sam's series is certainly stranger than the usual cute pics posted online by celebrities but clearly comes from the same place of love for his four-legged companions.

The Furnish-John Dogs

In the summer of 2020 David Furnish, husband of pop icon Elton John, posted an adorable photo of two small German Shepherd puppies on Instagram along with the hashtag #PuppyLove. The picture showed the couple's sons walking a puppy each. 'Introducing the newest members of the F-J Family,' wrote Elton on his Insta pages, but the family kept quiet about the dogs' names. On this day in 2012, *The Lion King* musical, with its songs written by Elton, became the highest grossing Broadway show, overtaking *The Phantom of the Opera*, which had held the top spot.

Gypsy & Picky

These were the childhood pets of British artist Ben Nicholson, who was born on this day in 1894. Nicholson came from true artistic stock. His father, William, was an artist, as was his mother, Mabel Pryde. In one of William's paintings, entitled *The White House, Sutton Veny* and painted in 1925, we see the family home in the background and their dogs, Gypsy and Picky (named after Picasso) in the foreground. Ben became one of Britain's most famous modernist painters.

Ringo

Talking about her dad's love of animals, especially dogs, Frank Sinatra's daughter, Tina, recalls asking him when she was a little girl where heaven was. 'Heaven is where all the animals go,' he told her. Growing up in Hoboken, New Jersey, Frank had not been allowed dogs as a child, and so he more than made up for it as an adult by having lots. He was especially fond of King Charles Spaniels. One of his dogs was called Ringo, but Ol' Blue Eyes was a big softie at heart and loved all the dogs he came across. On this day in 1966, he recorded *Strangers in the Night* for his album of the same name, which went on to reach No. 1 in the Billboard charts.

Y Chow Du

Nicknamed the 'Welsh Wizard', David Lloyd George, who was Prime Minister from 1916 to 1922, was a dog lover and was often seen out walking his St Bernard dog near his home in Churt, Surrey, once he retired. He was also keen on the Chow breed and named one Y Chow Du, which translates to 'the Black Chow'. His others were called Bandy, Beauty and Chong. Lloyd George was the Prime Minister when the British Parliament passed a 48-hour working week with a minimum wage on this day in 1919.

Dash

No prizes for guessing how the King Charles Spaniel got its name – correct, the toy spaniel was the favourite of King Charles II, whose own father, Charles I, also favoured the breed and so the young Charles had grown up surrounded by the little dogs who eventually took his name. Charles, who was known as the 'Merry Monarch', was something of a party boy and rumour has it he once decreed that Royal Spaniels should be permitted into any public building, including the Houses of Parliament. On this day in 1668, he appointed the first English poet Laureate, John Dryden. And while the names of Charles' dogs have been lost in time, we do know a later monarch, Queen Victoria, owned a Cavalier King Charles Spaniel called Dash.

Foxtrot

When it comes to genetics, dogs are close to wolves because they share a common ancestor and so the two species also share some of the same DNA. The two scientists credited with discovering the double-helix structure of DNA are James Watson and Francis Crick, who won a Nobel Prize in 1962 for their work. Fast-forward several decades and, on this day in 2003, the Human Genome Project, which sequenced 99 per cent of the human genome with 99.99 per cent accuracy, was completed. The only canine recipient of a Nobel prize is Foxtrot, who was awarded the Nobel Peace Prize in 2020 for his work with the UN World Food Programme, helping to relieve hunger and starvation in war-torn zones. Foxtrot lives in Banglasdesh.

15 APRIL

Mabel

Quirky-looking Mabel, who had an uncanny ability to know when she was on camera, was *Blue Peter*'s first-ever rescue dog. She joined the show in 1996 and was on screen for 14 years, making her the programme's longest-serving dog after Petra (*see* October 16) – and viewers loved her. Mabel had been a stray who was rescued from the streets of south-east London. She was just six months old when she became a *Blue Peter* pet, working alongside children's TV presenter Katy Hill, who celebrates her birthday today.

16 APRIL

Khala

Vegetarian since childhood, talented actor Anna Taylor-Joy is an animal lover who credits her dog as the reason she was talent-spotted at the age of 16. Anna explains how she was out walking Khala and, unusually, wearing high heels because she was off to a party, when a talent scout stopped her and helped launch her career as a model before she turned to acting. Anna, who was the star of the Netflix hit *The Queen's Gambit*, celebrates her birthday today.

17 APRIL

Cracker

Billy Fury, the 'Wondrous Place' rock 'n' roll singer and hit maker, had a rescue Boxer called Cracker who had belonged to the 1950s actor Diana Dors before moving in with Billy, who had a big soft spot for the breed. Cracker became something of a celebrity himself and even went on to star in a comic strip called *Don't Panic Girls* opposite Billy. You can see some great photos of the rocker with Cracker online. Born Ronald Wycherley on this day in 1940, Billy was dubbed the 'British Elvis' and was one of the UK's first rock stars.

18 APRIL

Fidèle

Yellow Labrador Retreiver Fidèle, who lived at the Côté Canal bed and breakfast in Bruges with owner Caroline Van Langeraet, became such a tourist attraction that he was featured in official tours of the city and even landed a cameo role in a major film. Fidèle liked to sleep on a windowsill facing the Groenerei canal and looked so peaceful snoozing there that tour boats would slow down to allow tourists to take his picture. He soon became the most photographed dog in the city and, according to his owner, would get fan mail and toys from as far away as America. Fidèle even had a cameo role in the hit thriller *In Bruges* starring Colin Farrell, which was released on this day in 2008.

19 APRIL

Mops

Mops was the name of Marie Antoinette's childhood dog who travelled from Austria to France with her when she left home at just 14 to be married off to the boy who would become Louis XVI of France. On this day in 1770, the pair were married by proxy (which simply means neither was physically present for the event) and, when Marie Antoinette arrived in France, she was told to relinquish all her possessions, including Mops. Happily, the dog and his mistresses were later reunited, and Mops lived a life of lavish luxury in the opulent palace of Versailles.

20 APRIL

Dog in the Sun

The Spanish surrealist painter Joan Miró was born in Barcelona on this day in 1893. Before turning to art, he worked as a bookkeeper to keep his goldsmith father happy, but he was so miserable in the job that his father eventually relented and sent him to art school. When he graduated at the age of 26, Miró moved to Paris, where he made friends with Pablo Picasso and started to paint in the Surrealist style. Dogs feature in a number of his paintings, either barking at the moon or playing. One of his most famous paintings is *People and Dog in Sun*, which he painted in 1949.

21 APRIL

Coco & Rhubarb

British film director Guy Ritchie, whose film *The Covenant* was released on this day in 2023, has two red Cocker Spaniels called Coco and Rhubarb, who both enjoy a visit to a traditional English pub while their human enjoys a quiet pint. Guy has made over 20 films, one of the best known being *Lock, Stock and Two Smoking Barrels*, which features a character called Dog.

22 APRIL

Jill the Dog

Canine actor Jill the Dog appeared as Verdell in the 1997 film *As Good As It Gets,* alongside film star Jack Nicholson, who celebrates his birthday today. In the film, Nicholson plays moody Melvin Udall, a misanthropic author who is rude to everyone he meets, including his neighbour Simon (Greg Kinnear). Melvin finds himself looking after Simon's dog, Verdell, and starts to show signs of softening, eventually forming a relationship with the only waitress Carol (played by Helen Hunt) who will still serve him in the café he frequents every day. The message of this uplifting drama is not to judge a book by its cover or write people – or, indeed, dogs – off when you don't really know them.

23 APRIL

Juno & Josie

Juno and Josie belong to baseball legend Mike Trout of the Los Angeles Angels and his wife, elementary school teacher Jessica. Mike even set up a joint Instagram account with the tag 'It's a dog's world' for the adorable dogs. On this day in 1914, the famous home of baseball team Chicago Cubs was opened at Wrigley Field, which was then known as Weeghman Park.

24 APRIL

Bo

President Obama, who was voted America's 44th President, had an extremely close relationship with Bo. The former President and his wife, Michelle Obama, had promised their daughters, Malia and Sasha, a puppy once they got to the White House. The first family chose Bo, a Portuguese water dog. Before long the whole family was in love with their dog. Writing about Bo, wife Michelle remembered how he 'was a constant, comforting presence in our lives, sauntering into one of our offices like he owned the place, a ball clamped firmly in his teeth.' Any activity – canine or otherwise – in the White House is always the subject of fierce press speculation. It was on this day in 1897 that the first dedicated White House correspondent, William Wallace Price, was assigned to the job.

Mr Famous

Photographed by the society photographer Cecil Beaton and appearing on countless magazine covers, Mr Famous starred with his owner, the actor Audrey Hepburn, in the film *Funny Face*, which was released in the UK on this day in 1957. Audrey was one of the first Hollywood stars to go everywhere with her beloved dog and so Mr Famous, who was a miniature Yorkshire Terrier, was never far from his owner's side, travelling the world with her and frequently seen either in her arms or riding on a basket on the front of her bicycle.

Bonnie

Blue Peter dog Bonnie took over from her mum, Goldie, in 1986 and was the only *Blue Peter* pet to be given one of the much-coveted *Blue Peter* badges. On her last day on the programme, she was presented with a specially made collar with a Gold *Blue Peter* Badge embedded in it.

Dodo

With his distinctive jowly face and portly figure, Winston Churchill was nicknamed the British Bulldog – not only because of his looks but also because he refused to surrender. And as it happens, the animal-loving wartime PM owned a bulldog of his own: a dog he called Dodo. Churchill led Britain to victory through the Second World War and his famous 'Never Give In' speech is still widely quoted to encourage people to keep going. On this day in 1941, German troops entered Athens to start the invasion of Greece.

28 APRIL

Dilyn

When this Jack Russell Terrier cross moved into the UK Prime Minister's official London residence at 10 Downing Street, his owners, Boris Johnson and his partner, Carrie, were not far behind. The Jack Russell is named after a Devon preacher, Parson John 'Jack' Russell, who was born in 1795. The pub in the North Devon village of Swimbridge, close to where he lived, is still called the Jack Russell. Parson Jack died on this day in in 1883.

29 APRIL

Blue

Tennis ace Andre Agassi saw the New Year in for 2023 in the company of his family and his beloved dog Blue and posted New Year greetings, which included a picture of the enormous dog lounging on the bed, to his fans. Agassi, an eight-time Grand Slam champion and an Olympic gold medallist, is married to another tennis superstar, Steffi Graf. The couple have had Blue since 2016 when he joined the family, and on New Year's Day, Agassi posted a picture of himself driving through the snow, his arm casually draped over Blue, a Great Dane, who was at his side in the front of the car. Today is Andre's birthday.

30 APRIL

Cabal

Cabal was a white German Shepherd rescue who found his way into the home and heart of award-winning writer Neil Gaiman, who reportedly first saw him shivering by the side of the road on this day in 2007. He brought the dog home with him, contacted the local shelter and drove the dog there so his owner could reclaim him. But in time, the shelter called Neil to see if he wanted to rescue the dog – originally called Buck – himself. 'I called him Cabal after King Arthur's dog who could see the wind,' wrote Neil. 'I'd never had a dog. I don't think he'd ever had a person. And we bonded.'

MAY

Trouble

She may have been known as the Queen of Mean in her lifetime but she wasn't mean when it came to making sure her little dog, Trouble, would continue to live the high life: Leona Helmsley left a staggering $12 million in her will to ensure Trouble would be well taken care of. The decision didn't please everyone, leading to a fight in the courts. Leona had married the American real-estate billionaire Harry Helmsley and helped him build a prestigious hotel chain. Harry once owned the Empire State Building, which formally opened on May 1 in 1931.

Purkoy

Henry VIII's ill-fated second wife, Anne Boleyn, had a little French lapdog called Purkoy (after the French word *pourquoi* meaning 'why?') The little dog has originally been given to Anne's cousin, Sir Francis Bryan, by Lady Lisle for New Year's as a kind of 'sweetener' because the Lisle family needed his help over some matter. But Bryan passed the dog on to the Queen and wrote to thank Lady Lisle saying, '... hearty thanks on my behalf for the little dog which was so well liked by the Queen it remained not above an hour in my hands, but her Grace took it from me.' On this day in 1536, that same Queen was arrested and imprisoned on charges of witchcraft, treason and adultery.

3 MAY

The Puppy Song

Singer-songwriter Harry Nilsson wrote plenty of whimsical songs but nothing quite as wistful (or correct) as the one that says having a dog is the key to happiness. 'The Puppy Song' appeared on Harry's 1969 album, which was called *Harry,* but had originally been written at Paul McCartney's request for the singer Mary Hopkin. Mary, who celebrates her birthday today, competed in the 1970 Eurovision Contest, finishing in second.

4 MAY

Bisbee & Mouchi

In March 2023, an English Setter called Bisbee entered the Guinness World Records for having the longest canine tongue in the world. Aged just three, Bisbee has a tongue that measures 9.49 cm (3.74 inches) and is longer than a lollipop. The previous holder of this record, Mochi, died in 2021 and was a St Bernard who had a tongue 18.58 cm (7.3 inch) long. *The Guinness Book of Records* as, it was previously known, was the brainchild of the industrialist Sir Hugh Beaver. A former managing director of the Guinness brewery, Sir Hugh was born on this day in 1890.

5 MAY

Bob & Freddy

Singing superstar Adele, who celebrates her birthday today, has two dogs – both Goldendoodles – who are named Bob and Freddy. The brothers joined Adele and her family in October 2021, when the 2013 Oscar-winning songwriter lovingly described them 'as a bit of a handful'. She said both dogs were responding well to training and explained that Freddy was called 'After Party Freddy' because he always wants to keep doing something when it has finished, and Bob was named Bob because he loves to be given a job.

6 MAY

Caesar of Notts

'I am Caesar. I belong to the King' was the inscription on the collar of Caesar of Notts, a Wire Fox Terrier belonging to King Edward VII, who died on this day in 1910. Born to the high life in 1898, Caesar was secretly referred to as 'Stinky' by courtiers, but the King loved him so much he slept on a chair alongside the royal bed and even had his own footman. And when the King died, it was Stinky who led the funeral procession, trotting along behind the coffin and taking precedent over heads of State and nine other kings, including George V. Germany's Kaiser Wilhem II was said to have been deeply offended.

7 MAY

Sandwich

Sandwich is the name Peter Parker (a.k.a. Spider-Man) gives to the stray dog he finds living on the streets while patrolling the city as the Marvel Comics superhero. He gains the dog's trust by giving it a sandwich which he has found in a dumpster, hence the name. Peter takes the dog home and tries to keep it hidden at his Aunt May's house. Unfortunately, his secret is short-lived and, when his aunt discovers Sandwich, she calls animal control. Since the first film in 2002, there have been nine Spider-Man films, eight of which are live action and one an animation. *Spider-Man 3*, starring Tobey Maguire, was released on this day in 2007.

8 MAY

Antis

Marking Victory in Europe Day, which took place on this day in 1945 and signalled the end of the Second World War in Europe, we remember a heroic dog. Antis was an Alsatian who served with Czech airman Václav Robert Bozděch in both the French Air Force and in the No. 311 (Czechoslovak) Squadron RAF in Britain. Antis was awarded a medal to honour his bravery of animals serving their country in the Second World War. Václav and Antis first met when Bozdech was shot down over no man's land between the French and German lines. He helped his injured partner to safety in an abandoned farmhouse, where he found the puppy all alone. They bonded and the duo ended up flying 30 combat missions together. They settled in England after Antis helped his master escape Czechoslovakia and a regimen that was punishing those who had served with the Western Allies.

Nana & Porthos

In the 1953 animated film *Peter Pan,* Brown Newfoundland dog
Nana is nursemaid dog to the Darling children and helps get
Wendy, John and Michael ready for bed before their parents, Mr
and Mrs Darling, go off to a party. The creator of Peter Pan, J.M.
Barrie, who was born on this day in 1860, was a dog lover and
based Nana on his own dog, a St Bernard called Porthos. The
Darlings have just three children, but James Matthew Barrie, who
was born in the small weaving town of Kirriemuir, Scotland, was
the ninth of ten children born to his hand-loom weaver father.

Bobbie the Wonder Dog

Scottish Collie mix Bobbie travelled over 4,105 km (2,500 miles) to find his way back to his owners after he was unwillingly left behind during a family trip to another state. Bobbie's family were visiting relatives in Wolcott, Indiana when Bobbie, then two, ran off. The heartbroken family spent hours looking for Bobbie but eventually gave up and returned to their Silverton, Oregon home without their beloved pet. Six months later, a scrawny Bobbie walked back through the door looking very much the worse for wear and like he must have walked the entire way. Bobbie became famous and played himself in the 1924 silent film *The Call of the West*. The film was released on this day in 1930.

Shep

The scene was set, the director shouted 'action' and the camera began to roll for another scene in the 1970s film *The Railway Children* when along came Shep... the black-and-white Collie plonked himself, literally, in the middle of the railway track to watch what was going on and had to be coaxed away by the actors starring in the film, which was was based on E. Nesbit's 1905 novel of the same name. Those stars included Jenny Agutter and Sally Thomsett. The film was shot in Haworth, Yorkshire and the dog 'extra' showed up on this day in 1970.

12 MAY

Kyte

Tervuren Belgian Shepherd and canine actor Kyte is best known
for her role as the third and longest-standing dog to play Wellard
in the long-running BBC TV soap *EastEnders* but she also played
the wolf that belonged to central character Maximus in the
Oscar-winning film *Gladiator*. *Gladiator* was released in the UK on
this day in 2000. The film, which starred Australian actor Russell
Crowe, was directed by Ridley Scott and won five Oscars in 2001,
including Best Actor and Best Picture.

13 MAY

Marvin

Marvin will be helping his owner, the model and actor Suki Waterhouse, get ready for a big day today because it is her boyfriend Robert Pattinson's birthday. The couple, who met through mutual friends in 2018, are both committed dog lovers and so Marvin, who is a Collie-Greyhound mix, probably thinks every day is his birthday. Suki, who has graced the covers of *Vogue* and *Elle*, says she's besotted by him. Robert, who was born in London in 1986, is the son of a vintage car dealer, Richard, and a modelling agency scout, Claire.

14 MAY

Missy

In July 2020, when the UK was in the grip of nationwide lockdowns, singer Olly Murs and his bodybuilder partner, Amelia Tank, rehomed a Shiba Inu dog, called Missy. Olly says that Missy has really helped prepare him and Amelia for parenthood, explaining, 'Having Missy has made me find my inner father, the inner dad in me that I never knew existed because I'd never really thought about children or anything like that.' The popular *The Voice* judge will be celebrating his birthday today.

15 MAY

Dougal

Dougal has the distinction of sharing his crib with the man widely regarded as America's foremost living artist, the painter and sculptor Jasper Johns. The wiry Greyhound mix dog faithfully follows Johns, who was born on this day in 1930, into his studio each morning to keep him company as he works. The Neo-Dadaist says his painted his best known work, *Flag* (1954–55), after having a dream about the American flag. The highest price paid for his work is $110 million, for his 48-star *Flag* (1958) in 2010.

16 MAY

Habañero Mountain Guy Kadashi Hart

The American singer-songwriter Pink and her husband, Carey Hart, win the award for the longest name given to any dog! The family introduced their pint-sized new rescue puppy via Twitter with a photo showing her children cuddling the new puppy and beaming. Pink, whose album *Hurts 2B Human* topped the US album charts on this day in 2019, is a keen animal advocate. The album went on to become No. 1 in eight more countries, including Canada, Australia, New Zealand and Switzerland, and was her third consecutive album to debut at No. 1 on the Billboard 200 chart.

17 MAY

Toto

The children's novel *The Wonderful Wizard of Oz* by L. Frank Baum was first published on this day in 1900. It was another 39 years before the story of Dorothy and her little dog, Toto, hit the silver screen with the release of *The Wizard of Oz*, starring Judy Garland and a female Cairn Terrier called Terry on 25 August 1939. New Yorker L. Frank Baum, who was originally a newspaper editor and reporter, was a prolific author, writing 14 Oz books, 41 other novels, 83 short stories, over 200 poems and at least 42 scripts.

18 MAY

Martha, Sally, Bernard & Mimi

On this day in 2011, John Lennon 's handwritten lyrics for the Beatles' song 'Lucy in the Sky with Diamonds' sold for $237,132 (£145,644) at auction in the US. John was a passionate animal lover and as a child, had a mixed-breed dog called Martha. In adulthood, John had two more dogs, Sally and Bernard, and then shared a little Terrier called Mimi (possibly after John's Aunt Mimi who raised him) with Yoko Ono and, in 1980, the couple gave their son, Sean, a dog as well. The song 'Lucy in the Sky with Diamonds' is from the band's 1967 album, *Sgt. Pepper's Lonely Hearts Club Band*, which had sold over 32 million copies worldwide by 2011.

19 MAY

Boatswain

There's no doubt that, when he wasn't busy shocking Middle England with his scandalous writings, love affairs and generally outrageous behaviour, the poet Lord Byron relished the time he spent with his animal menagerie, which included a fox, a parrot, five cats, a crow, a falcon, five peacocks, a goat with a broken leg and numerous horses. But of all his animals, the only one he honoured with their own tombstone was his beloved dog, Boatswain. Byron loved to gift his many lovers with a lock of his curly hair. Sadly, years later, DNA analysis of some 100 such gifts revealed most of them were actually canine, not human hair. For which we can probably thank Boatswain.

20 MAY

Nipper

Nipper was a dog from Bristol who served as the model for an 1898 painting by Francis Barraud, which was titled *His Master's Voice* and which went on to become of the world's best-known trademarks, several record companies using the iconic image of the dog and gramophone pairing. The little dog has a little brass plaque on the side of the bank building that was erected over his final resting place. The German-American inventor Emile Berliner, who was born on this day in 1851, is widely credited with inventing the first flat disc 'record'.

21 MAY

Bingo

Bingo was the Otterhound who starred as Sandy in the hit film *Annie*, released on this day in 1982. In the film, Sandy is a stray who we first see taking away an ear of corn from orphan Annie – but he returns it when she calls him back. Annie then assumes the dog must be looking for his parents, just like her, and decides to call the dog Sandy because his coat is the colour of sand. Bingo got the same VIP treatment as the other stars of the film and ate steak or prime rib every night. When the scene called for the dog to kiss her, the actor playing Annie, Aileen Quinn, would rub apple all over her face so he would lick it.

Pep

Richard Wagner, the German composer who gifted the world with so much classical music, including the epic *The Ring Cycle*, was a dog lover from childhood when he and his sister would rescue puppies. The musician liked to keep his dogs close by and became convinced that he had his own four-legged critic when his King Charles Spaniel, Pep, reacted to a new phrase or operatic composition. Pep would be in the study with the maestro as he composed, and Wagner admitted that he would check the dog for any emotional reactions – good or bad – before moving on to the next part of the composition. Wagner, who wrote 'Ride of The Valkyries', part of *The Ring Cycle* – four individual operas traditionally presented on consecutive evenings in a performance lasting about 15 hours – was born on this day in 1813.

23 MAY

Lily & Fritz

Melissa McBride, who plays Carol, a housewife turned fearsome zombie apocalypse survivor in the TV series *The Walking Dead*, is the owner of two dogs, Lily and Fritz. The Kentucky-born American actor and former casting director says she's a huge dog lover, and will be celebrating her birthday today. *The Walking Dead*, which premiered in October 2010, ran for 12 years and aired exclusively on the cable channel AMC. By season five, it was averaging 14.38 million viewers.

24 MAY

Brutus

Regarded as one of the greatest songwriters of all time, American musician and lifelong dog lover Bob Dylan was born in 1941 and celebrates his birthday today. Dylan has always had dogs and was known for touring with his pets. There were Labradors, a Beagle and a Collie, but his best-known dog was his Bullmastiff, Brutus. Dogs have featured in Dylan songs and even on his album covers, and in 2013, he released a children's book called *If Dogs Run* based on his lyrics from the song of the same name. The actor Michael Douglas tells a story about the time Brutus visited with Dylan and made a beeline for the caviar the Hollywood star had just ordered. Apparently, when Dylan realised what Brutus has done, he laughed and simply said, 'Far out...'

25 MAY

Fanny the Wonder Dog, Valerie, Albert & Gigi

When the British comedian Julian Clary first took to the alternative comedy circuit, he didn't face the audience alone because by his side he had a Whippet mix called Fanny the Wonder Dog. After Fanny came Valerie, another Whippet cross breed who was with Julian through his forties, before he welcomed Albert, who he says helped him settle into middle age, and then Gigi. In 2022, Julian published a memoir called *The Lick of Love: How dogs changed my life*, in which he tells the story of his life through his dogs and celebrates all the dogs he has loved to date. He celebrates his birthday today.

26 MAY

Sulamith Wülfing & Lily

A Chinese Crested Yorkshire Terrier mix who lived to the ripe old age of 18, Sulamith Wülfing was owned by the Fleetwood Mac singer Stevie Nicks, who once said she would like to be reincarnated as a dog. Nicks was heartbroken when Sulamith passed away and soon became the owner of a new dog called Lily. The rock star, who celebrates her birthday today, makes no secret of the fact the new arrival saved her life by bringing the joy and happiness that only a beloved dog can bring back into her world again.

27 MAY

Buddy

It's probably fair to say that singing superstar turned family man Robbie Williams is a dog lover since he had, at one time, at least seven in his family. Robbie, who was voted the Best Live Solo Artist Ever on this day in 2005, will often choose one of his dogs to go on tour and keep him company. Buddy is the latest four-legged addition to the Williams family. Buddy joined the family just days after their fourth child, a son called Beau, had been born to the same surrogate who carried their daughter Coco, and Robbie's wife, Ayda, introduced the new dog on Instagram with the hashtag #FullHouse.

28 MAY

Stickeen & Carlo

John Muir is the pioneering early environmentalist known as America's 'Father of National Parks'. Muir has his own small black dog called Stickeen, but he wrote about a friend's dog, a St Bernard called Carlo, in the book *My First Summer in the Sierra*, which was based on the sketches and journals of his 1869 stay in the craggy mountainous range that borders California and Nevada. Carlo was with him on that trip on loan from a friend, and so made it into Muir's story, immortalised in the pages of his book. It was on this day in 1892, in San Francisco, that John Muir formed the environmental group the Sierra Club.

29 MAY

Cookie

Melanie Brown, a.k.a. Scary Spice, is the owner of Yorkshire Terrier Cookie, who became the first-ever dog to enter the TV show *The Circle* when Mel B was a contestant. Cookie is pretty used to the limelight since he travels with the family, including on holidays to far-flung places, and so it's likely he won't be too far from Mel B's side when she celebrates her birthday today. Melanie and her Spice Girl bandmates scored nine UK No. 1 singles in the time they were performing together.

30 MAY

Ripken

If there is one thing that dogs are known for, it's playing fetch – though some are a little better at returning than others. One dog with no such trouble is Ripken, who is the official bat boy for Minor League Baseball club Durham Bulls. Trained by his owner, a former college baseball player, Ripken delights fans by running out to collect discarded bats from the field of play. Even better, Ripken is a talented fetcher across multiple sports, being used by his state American football team to fetch tees used for kicks. He's even been spotted doing his job while wearing a small camera, to give fans a dog-level view of the on-field drama. It was on this day in 1894 that baseball history was made, with Boston Beaneaters second baseman Bobby Lowe becoming the first person to hit four home runs in a Major League Baseball game.

Morse

Dogs are perhaps not known for their dancing abilities: something that rings true in the award-winning film *The Banshees of Inisherin*, which tells the story of a falling out between two lifelong friends in a remote island community off the west coast of Ireland. The film contained a wide variety of animal stars, from cart-pulling horses to little donkeys, but for dog lovers the finest performance came from Border Collie Morse. Owned by one of the on-set animal handlers, Morse plays Sammy, the beloved dog of Colm, one of the central characters. Colm has an ear for music, and one scene sees him sweetly holding his dog and gently dancing while he sings an old Irish song, 'Aghadoe'. Sammy seems somewhat less than impressed but suffers his doting owner's affections with good grace. Aside from Morse, the film stars Brendan Gleeson and Colin Farrell, whose birthday is today.

JUNE

1 JUNE

Maf

Remember how Rat Pack crooner Frank Sinatra was dotty about dogs (*see* April 11)? Well, he was so fond of dogs that he once rehomed a little white Poodle on behalf of Marilyn Monroe.

Monroe, who was born in Los Angeles on this day in 1926, was a dog lover too and named the little dog Maf, which was her jokey reference to the rumours that Frank had alleged connections to the Mafia. Frank had purchased the dog from actor Natalie Wood's mother, whose white poodle puppies went to the homes of many Hollywood stars.

2 JUNE

Sunny

Sunny is a Goldendoodle who belongs to Hollywood star Chris Hemsworth and his wife, Elsa Pataky. Sunny caused a panic in 2019 when he ran off while out on a walk in Australia's Byron Bay. The family, who are based in Byron Bay, posted all over social media to help find their beloved dog and the couple, along with their three children, were delighted to be reunited when Sunny was found. Chris starred as Eric the Huntsman in the blockbuster hit *Snow White and the Huntsman*, which was released in the United States on this day in 2012.

Pookie

Pookie was one of the small pack of Cairn Terriers owned by Edward VIII, the King who gave up the throne for his American love, Wallis Simpson, and married her on this day in 1937. Edward could not stay on as head of Church and State as well as marry his lover, socialite Wallis, because she was a divorcée. The couple's intention to marry caused a constitutional crisis, which resulted in Edward's abdication. Edward had reigned for less than a year and had never actually been crowned. The couple, who became known as the Duke and Duchess of Windsor, eventually moved with their dogs to live out their days in the South of France.

4 JUNE

Dusty

American actor, film-maker, humanitarian and activist Angelina Jolie is the owner of Rottweiler rescue dog Dusty, who was chosen by her children when the family visited the shelter. Dusty also has dog siblings in her new family, including an English Bulldog, two Pugs and a new puppy who joined the family in the summer of 2020. That same year, Angelina was also a producer on the film *The One and Only Ivan*, which stars a TV-loving stray dog called Bob who is befriended by circus gorilla Ivan. Angelina was born on this day in 1975.

5 JUNE

Champ

Actor Mark Wahlberg is proud owner of Pomeranian Champ, who regularly pops up on the *Ted* star's Instagram feed. Mark, who was a Calvin Klein model before turning his hand to acting, is also a producer and a rapper, and shot to fame as a member of the rap group Marky Mark and the Funky Bunch. He co-owns Champ with his wife, Rhea, and likes to celebrate his dog's birthday, as well as his own, which falls today for the Boston-born film star.

6 JUNE

Master Mongrel

Master Mongrel is one of a number of key dog characters who appear in the animated film *Kung Fu Panda*, which was released on this day in 2008. The story follows an out-of-shape Panda who must learn martial arts so that he can save the day. In order to make all the characters' movements as accurate as possible, the film's animators took kung-fu classes themselves.

7 JUNE

Shadow & Roosevelt

The Hanson brothers, who make up the chart-topping band Hanson, are a family who love dogs. Isaac has a dog called Shadow and Taylor's dog is Roosevelt. On this day in 1997, the band started a three-week long run at No. 1 on the UK singles chart with the song 'MMMBop'. One of the biggest debut singles of all time, the song reached No. 1 in 27 different countries. Lead singer Zac, who now has five kids of his own, was just 14 at the time the band had their breakthrough hit. The band is also celebrated by a dedicated Twitter account that likes to share photos of the Hanson trio with their dogs.

Jack & Jill

Titanic star Leonardo DiCaprio shared three huskies with his then girlfriend Camilla Morrone. In 2021, Leo took two of them, rescue dogs Jack and Jill, on the set the comedy/disaster film *Don't Look Up*, which he was filming in Boston. The dogs fell into icy water and were in danger until their famous owner dived in to pull them both out. Leo explained that, since they live in Southern California, the curious dogs had never seen a frozen lake before, got a little bit adventurous, went exploring and fell in. *Titanic*, in which Leo starred with British actor Kate Winslet, was premiered in London on this day in 1997.

9 JUNE

Lola

Bestselling crime novelist Patricia Cornwell is a big fan of dog rehoming and her own dog, Lola, is a rescue. One of the greatest gifts a dog can bring is their love and joy and so Patricia believes we can all learn a lot from our pets. 'Pay attention to the life in front of you,' she once tweeted. 'Do unto others. We are connected, all lives great and small.' Patricia, a former journalist, was working as a technical writer and computer analyst at the Office of the Chief Medical Examiner in Richmond, Virginia when she sold her first book, *Postmortem,* in 1990. Today is her birthday.

10 JUNE

Pompey

Pompey was the plucky little Pug who saved his noble master's life by alerting him to an assassination attempt while he slept. That master was no other than William I, Prince of Orange (also known as William the Silent), who lived between 1533 and 1584 and was a leader of the Dutch revolt against Habsburg Spain, which eventually led to independence for the Netherlands in 1648. On this day in 1928, a statue was erected to William at the Rutger's University College Avenue campus in New Brunswick, New Jersey. It was donated to commemorate the University's Dutch heritage.

Kevin

Game of Thrones actor and animal advocate Peter Dinklage lives in New York City with his wife and his young daughter – and his dog, Kevin. No stranger to dogs, in 2017, Peter campaigned to deter people from buying huskies simply because they resemble the Direwolves given to the Stark family children in the hit TV show. Instead, the actor who played the scheming but brilliant Tyrion Lannister, reminded people to commit to a dog as a member of their family and to 'adopt, not shop'. Kevin is a rescue and a mixed breed.

12 JUNE

Sawyer, Porscha, Lacey & Hannah

In February 2022, singing star Britney Spears introduced her Instagram followers to a tan-and-white dog originally from Maui, where she'd been visiting with her then fiancé and now husband Sam Asgari. The couple named the little dog Sawyer and set about settling him with his dog siblings: Porscha, a Doberman that Britney rehomed with Sam, a Maltese called Lacey and a Yorkie named Hannah. Britney was 'discovered' by music mogul Clive Calder, who sold his record company, Zomba, on this day in 2002 for $2 billion.

13 JUNE

Rico & Lola

Coronation Street actor and former Hear'Say singer Kym Marsh is the owner of Chihuahuas Rico and Lola. New dog, Rico, joined the family in 2018 and was looked after by Kym and her daughter. Kym says the new addition was named after the main character in Barry Manilow's hit song 'Copacabana', which tells the story of Rico, who takes a fancy to a showgirl called Lola. Writing in her *OK!* magazine column, Kym said, 'We already have a short-haired Chihuahua called Lola and we now have Rico too. He's very cute.' Kym's dogs will be helping her celebrate her birthday today.

14 JUNE

Frank

For dog lovers, it's not uncommon for our favourite actor in any film to be of the canine variety. There is a long list of four-legged performances that outshine those of their more celebrated human co-stars. But one of the finest examples has to be that of Frank, the wise-talking, street smart dog who (with a little encouragement) gives *Men in Black*'s two stars, Will Smith and Tommy Lee Jones, a crucial lead. Frank was originally played by a dog called Mushu, though the role in subsequent films in the franchise was played by other canine actors. *Men in Black: International* was released in cinemas on this day in 2019.

Ponto & Old Moll

The man accredited with breeding the foundation stock for the first English Setters was Sir Edward Laverack, who acquired two dogs, Ponto and Old Moll, in 1825 and developed their line into the English Setter we see today. Laverack lived in the village of Belton in North Lincolnshire. One famous fan of the English Setter was the Hollywood heartthrob actor Clark Gable, who played Captain Rhett Butler in *Gone with the Wind*.

Max

On the day that, in 1972, saw the release of David Bowie's classic album *The Rise and Fall of Ziggy Stardust and the Spiders from Mars*, we remember his dog, Max. The canine member of the Bowie entourage was notable for his heterochromia, a condition in which one eye colour is different from the other – something frequently attributed to the singer himself, though, in fact, his condition was anisocoria, a difference in the size of the pupil in each eye. That being said, the singer's fans loved the fact that Max – a Shih Tzu-Poodle mix – and David both had mismatched eyes.

Old Shep

'Old Shep' is the name of a song composed by American country singer Red Foley, who was born in Blue Lick, Kentucky on this day in 1910. For more than two decades, Foley was one of the biggest country stars in the world, selling 25 million records and helping to put the genre on the map after the Second World War. Venerated in the Country Music Hall of Fame, which called him 'one of the most versatile and moving performers of all time', he wrote 'Old Shep' about a dog he loved as a young child. Elvis Presley covered the song in 1956.

18 JUNE

Martha

Described as 'the hairiest Beatle' (though that's debatable in some of the band's later years) Martha was superstar and Beatles' frontman Sir Paul McCartney's dog. And so, far from being a love song to a woman, 'Martha My Dear' is actually Paul's love song to his faithful Old English Sheepdog companion and appears on their 1968 White Album. The Beatles remain the top-selling band of all time with 600 million units sold, with Martha playing her small part in their success. Paul McCartney celebrates his birthday on this day.

19 JUNE

Saucisse

Saucisse was a French Dachshund rescue who shot to fame in France as the protagonist of a book series – and also because he stood as a candidate in the mayoral elections of Marseille in 2001. Saucisse (which is French for 'sausage') also appeared in the TV series *Secret Story,* a reality show in the style of *Big Brother,* which first aired on this day in 2009. The little dog had been rehomed by a Marseille publishing house which specialised in detective novels, notably by the writer Serge Scotto, who used Saucisse as his mascot, made him the hero of many of his novels and gave him his name and claim to fame.

Skippy

On this day in 1837, Queen Victoria – who was the first royal patron of Battersea Dogs Home (as it was then known) – succeeded to the British throne. A keen supporter of animal welfare, Queen Victoria banned the (then) common practices of tail docking and ear cropping in the royal kennels. She was delighted to accept the Battersea patronage and before too long her son, Prince Leopold, became the first member of the Royal Family to rehome an animal from Battersea when he took home a little terrier called Skippy. Battersea has remained under royal patronage ever since – Her Majesty The Queen has been Battersea's patron since 2017, when she took over the mantle from the late Queen Elizabeth II.

21 JUNE

Fergus

Fergus is the little puppy who caught the attention of Their Royal Highnesses The Prince and Princess of Wales as they thanked mourners and well-wishers who had gathered in Windsor on 12 September 2022 to pay their respects to Her Majesty Queen Elizabeth II. On what was a sombre day for the Royal Family, an emotional Prince William spotted the little dog in the arms on an onlooker and, after greeting Fergus with a smile, told the assembled crowd, 'Doggies at this time are very important.' The future King of England was born on this day in 1982.

22 JUNE

Brandy

When she first met him, Brandy already had a job – as the 'watch' dog for a club called Talk of the Town. But for dog lover Judy Garland, it was love at first sight and the Hollywood actor was determined to 'liberate' Brandy, who became the last in a long line of her dogs. Judy, who was the first woman to win a Grammy award for Album of the Year, was just 47 when she died in London. She had won the prestigious award for her 1961 recording entitled *Judy at Carnegie Hall.*

23 JUNE

Alonzo

Rockabilly star Buddy Holly had a four-legged childhood pal
called Alonzo, a Collie cross. Buddy was born in Lubbock, Texas
during the Great Depression, into a musically talented family
with whom he had learned to play guitar and sing. He went on to
become the artist who defined the traditional rock 'n' roll line-up
of two guitars, bass and drums, and he was a major influence on
musicians who followed, on both sides of 'the pond', including Bob
Dylan, the Beatles, the Rolling Stones, Eric Clapton, the Hollies
and Elton John. On this day in 1990, Buddy's Gibson acoustic guitar
sold for £139,658 in a Sotheby's auction.

24 JUNE

Abu

Little Abu's owner is football legend Lionel Messi, who will be celebrating his birthday in one of the many homes (in Barcelona, Paris, Miami and hometown Rosario) that make up his real estate portfolio today. Abu is a Toy Poodle who joined the family in the autumn of 2020, becoming a dog sibling to Messi's gigantic Bordeaux Mastiff, Hulk, who was given to the Barcelona captain by his wife, Antonela Roccuzzo, in 2016. It's clearly a doggie tale of 'little and large' in the Messi household!

Calamity Jane

Calvin Coolidge was the 30th President of the United States, serving from 1923 to 1929. A country town lawyer with a reputation for being decisive, he was a popular president and so were his (mainly) white Collie dogs. One of his dogs – a Shetland Sheepdog – was given to the presidential family and had arrived with the name Diana but was soon renamed Calamity Jane after the famous American frontierswoman. The 1953 film *Calamity Jane* starred Doris Day, an actor whose own career was launched on this day in 1948 with the release of a film called *Romance on the High Seas*.

26 JUNE

Toulouse Lautrec

Toulouse Lautrec, Coco, Cinnamon, Strauss, Lafayette, Pignoli, Myron, Snape, Lily, Ophelia, Fawkes and Sirius – all 12 of these (mostly rescue) dogs belong to American singer Ariana Grande, who campaigns for animal rights and makes no secret of her preference for dogs over people. In one interview she even said, 'I love animals more than I love most people, not kidding!' Toulouse, who she rehomed from a rescue in 2013, often travels with the singer when she's on tour and even graced the cover of *Vogue* with his owner. When Cinnamon joined the Grande clan, Ariana wrote, 'She will be safe, spoiled and unconditionally loved!' Today it will be Ariana who is being spoiled, since it is her birthday.

27 JUNE

Sir Thomas

She never saw her dogs play with a ball or heard a joyous bark, but that did not stop deaf-blind Helen Keller from loving and owning dogs her whole life. In her 1933 essay, 'Three Days To See', Helen wrote that, if she suddenly had vision, she would 'look into the loyal and trusting eyes of my dogs... whose warm, tender and playful friendships are so comforting to me.' Sir Thomas, who was better known as Phiz, was a Boston Terrier given to Helen by her classmates at Radcliffe College. Helen, who was born on this day in 1880, became the first deaf-blind person to earn a Bachelor of Arts degree.

Molly & Maeve

The canine star of the 2005 hit film *Must Love Dogs* was played by two six-month-old Newfoundland puppies, called Molly and Maeve. Molly carried most of the role, but Maeve performed the water scene where Sarah, played by actor Diane Lane, and her dog 'Mother Teresa' (played by Maeve) jump out of a boat to rescue Jake (actor John Cusack, who celebrates his birthday today). The two puppies do appear together at the end of the film and, in a perfect dog-loving twist, the writer, producer and director, Gary David Goldberg, rehomed both puppies once shooting was over!

29 JUNE

Bummer & Lazarus

Bummer and Lazarus were two strays whose complete devotion to each other captured the hearts of San Francisco's residents in the 1860s. At that time, the city had strict anti-stray dog policies, but Bummer and Lazarus were allowed to do as they pleased. The newspapers reported on the two companions and everyone admired their great love for each other. The dogs were welcomed at all local eateries and hostels and, when an overzealous city official unwisely captured Lazarus on 14 June in 1862, citizens demanded his release. The city supervisor eventually gave in and declared the two dogs could roam where they wanted. The *San Francisco Bulletin* described them as 'two dogs with but a single bark, two tails that wagged as one'. The city of San Francisco was founded on this day in 1776.

The Blondin Terriers

The greatest of all rope-walkers, daredevil Charles Blondin (real name Jean-François Gravelet) absolutely loved dogs and always seemed to have a number of them weaving in and out of his feet. The French-born acrobat, famous for walking across the mighty Niagara Falls on a tightrope, renamed the house he bought in 1889 'Niagara House' and, according to the Blondin Memorial Trust, lived there happily with his daughter, Adele, as well as the widow of a friend, a coachman, a servant and various black-and-tan Terriers. By the time The Great Blondin, as he was known, gave his final performance in 1896, it was estimated he had crossed the Falls 300 times – and walked more than 16,090 km (10,000 miles) on his tightrope, every one of them without a net or safety harness.

JULY

1 JULY

Wheely Willy

Wheely Willy is a paraplegic Chihuahua who is the subject of two bestselling children's books and, along with his owner, has toured the world, even bringing Japanese royalty to their knees, with the aim of spreading awareness for those with disabilities. His owner wrote a children's book, *How Willy Got His Wheels,* which was published on this day 1998.

Dogmatix

Dogmatix is a fictional character from the comic book series *Asterix*, where he is Obelix's companion dog. The little White Terrier with long rabbit-style ears, whose English name is a clever pun on the words 'dog' and 'dogmatic', first appeared in the edition *Asterix and the Banquet*. Of all present-day dog breeds, the one that looks most like Dogmatix is the West Highland White Terrier, or 'Westie', as they are affectionately known. On this day in 2021, *Dogmatix and the Indomitables* was first released – a spin-off TV show from the original series featuring Dogmatix as the lead character.

Muttley

Wacky Races was an American animated TV series for kids that featured 11 different cars racing against each other in various road rallies throughout North America to try to win the title of World's Wackiest Racer. For the generation that grew up watching the show on Saturday mornings, one of the most memorable characters was Muttley – the four-legged sidekick to the villain of the series, driver Dick Dastardly. In fact, these two were so popular they got their own 1969 spin-off show called *Dastardly and Muttley in Their Flying Machines*. In real life, on this day in 1886, Karl Benz officially unveiled the Benz Patent-Motorwagen, the world's first purpose-built car.

4 JULY

Prada

Canine actor Prada the Beagle was best known for his role as one of the dogs who played Porthos in *Star Trek Enterprise*. Prada also played the lead character, Lou, in the film *Cats & Dogs*, voiced by actor Tobey Maguire. *Cats & Dogs* was released on this day in 2001.

5 JULY

Angie

Esther Williams achieved fame not only for her competitive swimming but also as an actress, appearing in a series of what became known as 'aquamusicals', showing off her skills with elaborate performances including displays of diving and synchronised swimming. But beyond swimming and acting, Esther's passion was dogs, and many glamorous photographs show the star playing with animals, including her own cocker spaniel, Angie. Esther's brand of marine glamour was echoed on this day in 1946, when a model called Micheline Bernardini modelled the very first (and at that time risqué) bikini at a swimming pool in Paris. The two-piece, named 'bikini' by the man who designed it, a French engineer called Louis Réard, was such a hit that Louis quit his other work, opened a bikini shop and ran it for the next 40 years.

6 JULY

Riggs & Roxy

American funny man Kevin Hart has two rescue dogs – Roxy, a Doberman Pinscher, and Riggs, a miniature Doberman. The comedian has said he was never a dog person until his wife, Eniko Parrish, introduced him to the joy of living with dogs, and since then, he has not looked back, admitting he likes to give both dogs a treat whenever he leaves the house or comes home. Riggs is named after Mel Gibson's character in the action film series *Lethal Weapon* and today is People's Choice Award winner (2021) Kevin's birthday.

7 JULY

Davie, Bruce & Mountain Boy

The 28th US President was Democrat and dog lover Woodrow Wilson. President Wilson had three dogs during his tenure at the White House: an Airedale Terrier named Davie, a Bull Terrier named Bruce and a Greyhound called Mountain Boy. During the First World War, he drafted almost three million young men to serve in the armed services. The very first military draft started on this day in 1863 – exemptions cost $300.

8 JULY

Max & Duke

These two are the stars of the 2016 blockbuster hit *The Secret Life of Pets*, which earned $875 million at the box office, making it the sixth highest-grossing film of that year. Without giving too much away, Max the Terrier is a pampered but neurotic uptown pooch living his best life in lower Manhattan, where he is loved and adored by his owner, Katie. But Max's perfect world is rocked when Katie comes home one day with Duke, a giant hairy rescue dog who is a Newfoundland mix. The two vie for Katie's attention but, when they find themselves lost in the city, they must put their differences aside and work together to find their way home. The film – the first in the franchise – was released on this day in 2016.

9 JULY

Archie

Of all the quotes he's remembered for, a dog lover's favourite is usually the time pop artist Andy Warhol said, 'I never met an animal I didn't like.' Andy grew up a cat lover but, in 1973, his then boyfriend, Jed Johnson, persuaded him to get a dog. The couple brought home a dark brown Shorthaired Dachshund they called Archie and, within days, Andy was besotted with the new addition to the family, taking him to his studio, to art openings and to Ballato's Restaurant on Houston Street. Archie was always on Andy's lap being hand-fed tasty treats, and Andy would hide him under his napkin if he thought he'd be spotted and thrown out. Andy had his first solo show on this day in 1962.

DJ Oliver & Pepe

DJ Oliver is a Maltese-Poodle mix with a very famous chart-topping owner called Rihanna. Pomeranian Pepe is his dog brother who, according to reports, Rihanna rehomed in West Hollywood. She brought the little dog home and decided to keep him. The two little dogs now have a two-legged brother with the arrival of Rihanna's son, who she named Fine. On this day in 1973, the Bahamas gained full independence within the Commonwealth of Nations. Barbados, which is Rihanna's home state, had already trailed the way, becoming independent in 1966.

Donnchadh the Bloodhound

Donnchadh the Bloodhound was owned by Scottish warrior Robert the Bruce, who was the King of Scotland. The courageous hound bravely protected his master as he fought for Scottish independence. While Robert was in hiding, opposing forces captured the dog and used him to lead them to Robert's location, but then, when they went in to attack Robert, stories say that the dog turned to his defence, saving his master's life. Robert was born on this day in 1274.

12 JULY

The Dingo

The Dingo is a wild dog believed to have arrived in Australia about 4,000 years ago but its origins go way back to earlier breeds of domestic dogs in Southeast Asia, so it is thought the breed first came to Australia with Asian seafarers. Before long, Dingoes were working alongside Aboriginal people, helping them to catch small animals for food. On this day in 1971, the Australian Aboriginal flag, which has the same legal and political status as the country's national flag, was flown for the very first time.

Moonie

Canine actor Moonie, who was also known as Moondoggie, was the Chihuahua who played Bruiser Woods in the *Legally Blonde* franchise, starring alongside Reese Witherspoon. Like his owner, Elle Woods, the Harvard law student played by Reese, Bruiser Woods was a Gemini vegetarian, but in real life Moonie was a much-loved dog who lived to the ripe old age of 18. *Legally Blonde*, which grossed $141.8 million at the box office and made Reese a household name (and Bruiser too, among dog lovers), was released on this day in 2001.

14 JULY

Sassafras

Puppies – both with and without superpowers – have featured in the pages of the Marvel Comic books for decades and Sassy, the Dog Filled With Fear, was the little dog that belonged to Hank McCoy, better known as the X-Men's Beast. During his time in the pages of *Defenders,* Beast and Sassy chased cars and scrapped over their favourite dog toys together. On this day in 2000, the first blockbuster hit, *X-Men*, starring Hugh Jackman as Logan/Wolverine and Halle Berry as Storm, was released.

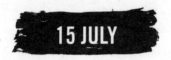

15 JULY

Bianca & Suzie Dog

American actor, model, author and animal activist Beth Ostrosky Stern first learned about animal nutrition when she was looking after her English bulldog, Bianca. Beth decided to write a book sharing her experiences and opinions on dog ownership. Beth has always had dogs in her life and jokes that her parents' 'first born' was a Collie mix named Suzie Dog.

16 JULY

Astro & Gorby

It's no surprise that that the first man to walk on the Moon would call his dog Astro – after the stars. Belonging to Neil Armstrong, Astro was a Rottweiler and, when fellow astronaut Sunita Williams signed up for a stint on the International Space Station, she took with her for company a cardboard cut-out of her little Jack Russell dog, Gorby, dubbed 'Flat Gorby' by the crew. On 16 July 1969, the Apollo 11 Saturn V space vehicle which took Armstrong to the Moon lifted off at 9.32 a.m. EDT from the Kennedy Space Center's Launch Complex and witnesses reported that Astro was with Armstrong's family at the centre.

The Lady & The Tramp

No self-respecting dog lover can hear the name Walt Disney without thinking about the animated classic *Lady and the Tramp*, which tells the story of the relationship between a pampered Cocker Spaniel called Lady and a tough stray called Tramp. Lady finds herself stranded on the streets after her owners have a baby and street-smart Tramp not only befriends and protects her but soon falls in love. Remember the scene where the two dogs share a strand of spaghetti? There's a reason this film, which was based on a story published in *Cosmopolitan* magazine called 'Happy Dan, the Cynical Dog' is a classic ... On 17 July in 1955, Walt Disney opened Disneyland in Anaheim in California.

Schoep

Dog lovers across the world shed a tear on hearing of the death on this day in 2013 of a much-loved rescue dog called Schoep, who became famous overnight after his devoted owner, John Unger, shared a photo showing the elderly dog cradled in his arms in Lake Superior, having hydrotherapy for his arthritis. John explained this was their evening ritual because it provided some relief for the dog's pain. The photo went viral and donations worth $10,000 flooded in, which meant Schoep, a German Shepherd mix that John had rehomed as an eight-month-old puppy, could have advanced laser therapy treatments to reduce swelling and pain. Schoep lived to 20 and the tender photo of the two of them together can still bring a tear to the eye.

Freddie Mercury

Little Freddie Mercury is an Instagram star who now has over 30,000 followers – and rising. The abandoned Chihuahua mix was found under a car in Los Angeles but now has a happy home with owner Angela Adan. The little dog survived two broken legs, which never properly healed, and has an overbite, just like his namesake, but is loved and adored by Angela. The original Freddie Mercury was, of course, the lead singer of the rock band Queen, whose guitarist, the quieter astrophysicist and animal champion Brian May, celebrates his birthday today.

Peritas

While not a breed we might recognise today, Peritas, who was the favourite dog of Alexander the Great, looked like a Dogue de Bordeaux, a Mastiff or even, according to one description, a Neapolitan Mastiff. In other words, this was no little dog! According to legend, the faithful hound went everywhere with his master and even saved his life during one battle, after which the former King of Macedonia was so grateful that he honoured his dog by naming a city after him. Historians estimate that Alexander was born on this day in 356 BC.

Trump

The painter and satirist William Hogarth was known for his love of dogs and his Pug, Trump, featured in his self-portrait *The Painter and his Pug*, now part of the Tate collection. It is said that, in his paintings, Trump serves as an emblem of the artist's own pugnacious nature. The Tate Britain was opened on this day in 1897 by the then Prince of Wales and Queen Victoria's second child and eldest son, Albert, who was known as Bertie. And in royal tradition, he too was a big dog lover.

22 JULY

Cosmo the Spacedog

Though names such as Spiderman, Iron Man and Doctor Strange may take the headlines, for dog lovers, the best character in the Marvel comic universe – spanning book, film, television and more – is Cosmo the Spacedog. Graced with telepathic abilities, Cosmo the chief of security at the Knowhere space station and has been at the centre of many escapades in his various guises across the Marvel franchise. On the big screen, a female version of the character has even made a cameo in the global hit series of films, *Guardians of the Galaxy*. This day in 2019 saw the Marvel film *Avengers: Endgame*, featuring characters from across the Marvel universe including *Guardians of the Galaxy*, become the highest-grossing film of all time.

23 JULY

Pal

The American industrialist Henry Ford, the founder of the Ford Motor Company, was the man who made the motor car accessible to the masses by introducing the moving assembly-line method of production to car manufacturing. In a striking 1928 portrait shot, it's not his family or co-workers posing alongside him but a German Shepherd dog, called Pal. German Shepherds were kept onsite at the Detroit-based company, but Henry's daughter, Edsel, also had one as a pet. The Ford Motor Company sold its very first car on this day in 1903 and the business magnate was worth a staggering $188 billion (today's equivalent) by the time he died in 1945.

24 JULY

Beethoven

And then along came *Beethoven* – one of the all-time classic dog films that captured hearts around the world. The film, which was released on this day in 1992, ushered in a golden age of films in the 1990s that took Hollywood by storm. The film tells the heart-warming story of the bonds that form between the Newton family and their newly rehomed puppy. As Beethoven grows, he helps the Newton children overcome life's obstacles as they, too, come of age. Although the role was originally written for a Golden Retriever, Beethoven was a St Bernard mountain dog and played by a dog called Chris, who had 12 doubles for stand-in scenes.

Lady & Mush

Singer Karen Carpenter had two dogs: Lady, a Belgian Shepherd, and Mush, who was a Samoyed. Karen and her brother, Richard, who together made up the Carpenters, had hit after hit in the 1970s and made one of the biggest-selling albums of the decade with their compilation of these hits, *The Singles: 1969–1973*. On this day in 1970, the Carpenters started a four-week run at No. 1 on the US singles chart with their hit '(They Long to Be) Close to You'.

26 JULY

Poppy & Ruby

Actor Sandra Bullock, who will be celebrating her birthday today, has a history of offering a home to dogs with special needs. The Oscar-winning star of *Bird Box* and *Ocean's Eight* rehomed Poppy, a Chihuahua-Pomeranian mix who lost a leg in a car accident, and Ruby, who had lost two legs. The actor once said she welcomes 'any dog that is missing something'. She is now proud owner of a poodle rescue.

27 JULY

Owney the Postal Dog

Owney was an unofficial mascot for the US Postal Service in the late 1800s and, on this day in 2011, had a commemorative stamp dedicated to his memory. The little Terrier mix travelled 225,300 km (140,000 miles) across 48 different states and around the world, and liked sleeping on mail bags. He had been owned by a clerk at the Albany post office in New York, who would often bring little Owney to work with him. When he left the service, his owner felt Owney would always be happier at work than at home and his colleagues agreed – arguing that Owney also brought good luck to everyone who worked with him. The trains he travelled on never crashed and so he was welcomed wherever he went.

Hooch

Hooch is the name of the French Mastiff dog (real name Beasly) who played opposite actor Tom Hanks in the film *Turner & Hooch*. Beasly was just 17 months old when he landed the role, which he shared with two other dogs, including a stunt double called Igor. The producers looked at 50 different breeds before settling on the Dogue de Bordeaux, declaring him big – but not too big. In interviews, Tom explained he would spend days playing with all the dogs who played Hooch because otherwise, once filming started, they would just keep their eyes on their trainer. In the film, which was released on this day in 1989, Detective Scott Turner, played by Hanks, takes the dog in as the only witness to his owner's murder. The dog wreaks total havoc in his life but also leads him to the love of his life: the local veterinarian.

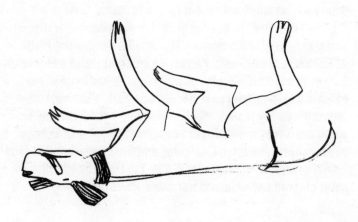

29 JULY

Krypto the Superdog

Krypto the Superdog is a DC comics hero who is most closely linked with Superman. The duo are the best of friends, share the same superpowers and are pretty much inseparable as they fight crime, side by side, in the city of Metropolis. Krypto is a white dog of an unspecified breed. In the animated film *DC League of Super-Pets*, which was released on this day in 2022, Superman and the rest of the league get kidnapped by Lex Luthor and it is up to Superdog Krypto to rescue them. Luckily, he finds a group of shelter dogs with hidden superpowers and convinces them to help.

30 JULY

Lou

Cats & Dogs is the 2001 animated comedy film which exposes the top-secret, high-tech espionage war going on between the two species about which their human owners have no clue. Lou is the main protagonist, a Beagle voiced by Tobey Maguire in the first film. At the end of that film, Lou is adamant he will never become an agent, but by the time the sequel, *Cats & Dogs: The Revenge of Kitty Galore*, is released on this day in 2010, he has become the head of D.O.G.S. (and is now voiced by Neil Patrick Harris).

Rum

Rum was a Dorgi, which is a cross between a Dachshund and a Welsh Corgi. This mix came about when one of Corgis owned by the late Queen Elizabeth II mated with a Dachshund called Pippin belonging to her sister, Princess Margaret. The sisters went on to own many more Dorgis, one of whom was called Rum and belonged to Margaret. Queen Elizabeth II was a patron of Battersea and made two official visits: one in 1991 and another in 2015. But the reason Rum is today's star dog is that, on this day in 1970, the Royal Navy stopped the practice of an official daily rum ration for every sailor. The last day the sailors got their rum ration became known as Black Tot Day.

AUGUST

1 AUGUST

Cora

When the first English settlers arrived in Newfoundland and Labrador, which is the most easterly province in Canada, they brought with them their dogs. And because most of these first settlers were fishermen from South West England, the breed they brought was a cross breed, which became known as the St John's Water Dog and which is the forbear of the modern Labrador. These dogs were brilliant at retrieving nets, lines and ropes, and would even dive to retrieve fish that had slipped from their hooks. So now you know why your Lab loves water! Cora is one of these early Lab ancestors and is depicted in a painting by the English Georgian artist Charles Joseph Hullmandel. The Georgian era started on this day in 1741 when King George I took the throne.

Heen

Japanese animation masters Studio Ghibli produce breathtaking, magical films. Often set in fantastical make-believe worlds, the films frequently feature cats in various forms, but the animators have turned their hand to creating some very sweet canine characters too – and perhaps none are as familiar to some dog owners as Heen, from the film *Howl's Moving Castle*. Heen is scruffy and lazy – but he has a good heart. The studio's film *Castle in the Sky* was released on this day in 1986.

Indiana

One of the superpowers that dogs possess is the way they can encourage us when we're feeling low, or inspire us when we're short of ideas. And an Alaskan Malamute called Indiana did exactly that when his owner – filmmaker George Lucas – was writing what would become one of the biggest film franchises of all time, *Star Wars*. Lucas has said that his sweet dog was his constant companion as he was writing. As good natured as he was fluffy, Indiana got this owner thinking and eventually inspired him to give the dashing, swashbuckling character Han Solo a sidekick: a big, hairy, faithful companion called Chewbacca. Lucas's film *American Grafitti* premiered at the Locarno International Film Festive on this day in 1973.

Red Dog

Red Dog was a Kelpie-Cattle cross who, in 1975, travelled independently around the Pilbara mining region of Western Australia after his truck-driver owner passed away. He made friends with many locals, uniting a disparate community as he searched for his owner, and had such an impact on the people whose lives he touched that a film was made to tell his story and released on this day in 2011. Described as an endearing, funny and idiosyncratic tale of human folly and dog wisdom, *Red Dog* is a true family film.

Ashley Whippet

On this day in 1974, Ashley Whippet and his owner, Alex Stein, ran onto the baseball field before a Dodgers game and stunned fans with the dog's incredible frisbee act. The dog – described as the Michael Jordan of dog athletes – became the first 'disc dog' and the originator of a sport grew in popularity with a tournament named after him. He went on to perform at the Super Bowl, at the White House and on television, and was even featured in a movie. When he died, Ashley was honoured by a glowing tribute in the pages of the prestigious *Sports Illustrated* magazine. Ashley had been named because of his ash colour and also in honour of Ashley Wilkes, one of the characters in the American Civil War film *Gone with the Wind*.

George

One of the singers at the 1970 Festival for Peace, which took place at New York's Shea Stadium on this day, was the American singer Janis Joplin, who loved dogs – so much so she would rehome strays and take them on tour with her. Janis had a Collie called George who was never far from her side. The Festival for Peace was a star-studded event staged to raise funds for anti-war political candidates. Another famous singer taking part was fellow dog lover Dionne Warwick, who has had dogs from the age of eight and who says animals are one of her true loves in life. 'They know they have my love and I know I have theirs. Dogs have always been a part of my life and always will be,' she adds.

7 AUGUST

Leo, Cleo, Johnny & Berkley

These four rescue dogs belong to big-hearted Hollywood actor Charlize Theron, who will be celebrating her birthday today. The South African-born actor has had a long and varied career and is noted for her versatility. Charlize is adamant that rehoming pets is 'the only way to go' and often shares photos of herself snuggling up to her dogs with her seven million Instagram followers. She explains her devotion to dogs and all animals saying, 'As a kid growing up on a farm in rural South Africa, my only friends were animals.'

Oldie

Odie, the comic strip dog, appears in the *Garfield* comics and films as the pet of Jon Arbuckle. Odie's first appearance was on this day 1978. In the comics, Odie is introduced by Jon's friend and roommate, Lyman, but in the film version, the story changes and Jon rehomes Odie as a rescue from a vet centre. Odie is a depicted as a lovable, kind, yellow-furred, brown-eyed Beagle who is Garfield's best friend. He can communicate complete sentences in barks and is described by Garfield as 'honest, true blue and decent'. He has a huge tongue and often drools huge puddles. In the comic of 26 August 2007, Garfield tries to find out what breed Odie is by looking him up in a dog breeds book and concludes, 'he's pure clown'.

Stella

Stella belongs to Chicago-born actor Gillian Anderson, who grew up in England and Michigan. Stella is an Australian Labradoodle and was introduced to the public via Instagram with Gillian writing, 'Meet my new gf, Stella'. Gillian shot to fame playing Dana Scully in the TV sci-fi show *The X-Files*, which ran from September 1993 to May 2002 and which was revived for a short tenth season in 2016. Gillian, who more recently played Margaret Thatcher in Netflix series *The Crown*, celebrates her birthday today.

Muttnik

Muttnik was the name of a small Wire Fox Terrier who belonged to the Canadian-American psychotherapist Nathaniel Branden, a pioneer in the field of self-esteem. Nathaniel was also the partner of one of America's foremost authors, the novelist Ayn Rand, whose book *Atlas Shrugged* depicts a dystopian United States in which private businesses suffer under the weight of increasingly burdensome laws and regulations. The book's two main characters are Dagny Taggart, a railroad executive, and her lover, steel magnate Hank Rearden. And while Ayn's story was one of fiction, members of the Amalgamated Association of Iron and Steel workers went out on strike on this day in 1901.

Esmerelda, Kenobi & Rommel

Esmerelda is a chocolate Labrador whose owner, actor Anne Hathaway, prefers to rehome, which means Esmerelda's brother, Kenobi, who is a Spaniel-Terrier mix, is a rescue too. Kenobi is named after Anne's favourite *Star Wars* character, Obi-Wan Kenobi. The actor herself was the star of the *Princess Diaries* franchise including *The Princess Diaries 2: Royal Engagement,* which was released on this day in 2004. In the films, Rommel is the dog that belongs to Princess Mia's Grandmother. He loves living the high life with her in New York's Plaza Hotel.

12 AUGUST

Boy & Xanto

Winnaretta Singer, a.k.a. Princesse Edmond de Polignac, was the American-born heiress to the Singer sewing machine fortune and liked to use her money to fund many causes. She hosted a musical salon in her Parisian home, and thus supported the careers of the French composers Debussy and Ravel. Debussy liked dogs, and Boy, a Fox Terrier, and Xanto, a Collie, both belonged to him. Interestingly, Debussy's mother was a seamstress, his father a salesman and china shop owner. Debussy moved to Paris at the age of 10, the city where Winnaretta lived most of her life. On this day in 1851, her father, Isaac, was granted a patent for his sewing machine.

13 AUGUST

Beth, Bluebell, Sugar & Honey

Their Majesties The King and Queen are well known for their love of dogs and, together, the royal couple have two Battersea rescues: Jack Russell Terriers Beth and Bluebell. The King may have been raised with Corgis and Dorgis, but His Majesty has seemingly much admired the character of Jack Russell dogs. Even as a child, there were dogs in the royal nursery and, at that time, the then Prince had a playmate called Sugar, who was the twin sister to his grandmother's Corgi, who was called Honey. Clearly someone in the royal household had a penchant for giving their dogs (literally) sweet names.

Jackson & Roman

These two Labradoodles belong to Hollywood actor Halle Berry, who celebrates her birthday today. Born to an American father and an English mother, Halle started her career as a model before becoming an actor and landing her breakthrough role in the romantic comedy *Boomerang*, playing opposite Eddie Murphy. Halle is a huge animal lover and even had a hand in training her canine co-stars in the 2019 action thriller *John Wick: Chapter 3 – Parabellum*, which stars Keanu Reeves. In the film, her character, Sofia, meets John for the first time with her two Belgian Malinois dogs, as she asks, 'Are you a dog person, John?' The two dogs were played by five different canine actors: Santana, Tai, Sam 7, Boyca and Ikar.

15 AUGUST

Dandie Dinmont

The writer and historian Sir Walter Scott, who was born on this day in 1771 in a small flat in Edinburgh's Old Town, holds the distinction of creating the only fictional character to have given their name to a breed of dog. In his novel, *Guy Mannering*, the character Dandie Dinmont is a rough but friendly farmer from the Liddesdale Hills who owns a pack of Terriers. In real life, the Dandie Dinmont has a softly curved, rather than an angular body, large eyes, short legs and a domed head crowned by a silky topknot.

Michelangelo's Pomeranian

Michelangelo's Sistine Chapel ceiling is one of the truly great masterpieces of Renaissance art, a riot of colour and drama spread out over a canvas some 120 feet long, high about the floor of the chapel itself. It's a breathtaking work – one that took the artist several years to complete. It's said that around five million people flock to see the painting each year, but can you imagine being there at the time to watch such an important piece being created? If legends are to be believed, Michelangelo did have one such witness – his Pomeranian, who stories say would sit on a silk cushion while his owner worked, doubtless paying no attention and bored by the whole affair. It was on this day in 1501 that Michelangelo was awarded the contract to create his other great work in Florence, the statue of David.

17 AUGUST

Isis & Pharaoh

It rare to see any scene in the TV period drama hit series *Downton Abbey* where the head of the Crawley family, Robert Crawley, is not accompanied by one or more of his Golden Labradors, who were named Isis and Pharaoh. In fact, the bond between master and his dogs is so powerful that almost every one of the 52 episodes, aired over six series, had an introduction showing the dogs walking besides Lord Grantham. Pharaoh was played by a canine actor called Roly and Isis by one called Ellie. The creator of *Downton Abbey*, the novelist Julian Fellowes, was born on this day in 1949.

Keon

The Guinness World Record for the longest tail on a dog currently belongs to an Irish Wolfhound called Keon, whose tail (measured and verified by a vet) runs 76.7 cm (30.2 inches) long from the tip to the base, excluding any hair. His name might mean 'courageous warrior' but Keon's family, who live in Belgium, described him as a gentle giant. Dog lovers say Irish Wolfhounds have a heart as big as the rest of them and, just like Keon's owners, describe the breed as noble, sensitive and very easy going.

Gigot

Gabrielle 'Coco' Chanel wasn't just famous for revolutionising the way women dressed by freeing them of corsets and lace frills; the trailblazing fashion designer was also a dog lover. She called her Great Dane dog Gigot and lived with her on the French Riviera. Chanel, who favoured tailored suits and men's trousers for women, was born in Saumur, in the Loire Valley, France, on this day in 1883.

20 AUGUST

Pomsky

A cross between a Siberian Husky and a Pomeranian, Pomsky belongs to someone who makes no secret of the fact he is a huge dog lover: the TV personality, entrepreneur and record executive Simon Cowell. The *Pop Idol, X Factor* and *Britain's Got Talent* judge rehomed Pomsky in the summer of 2022 and the duo made their red carpet debut during the live semi-finals for Season 17 of *America's Got Talent* at the Sheraton Passadena Hotel. On this day in 2003, Madam Tussauds in London opened an interactive *Pop Idol* display with a speaking waxwork of Simon, whose comments included, 'That was the worst performance I have ever seen!'

Bob

Bob, who is voiced by actor Danny DeVito, is a TV-loving scrappy stray dog who has made the mall his home in the film *The One and Only Ivan,* which was released on this day in 2020. The Disney film is about an easy-going gorilla called Ivan (voiced by actor Sam Rockwell) who lives with his elephant and dog friends at the Exit 8 Big Top Mall and Video Arcade. Based on the novel of the same name, which was written by K.A. Applegate, the film was shot at the Southgate Shopping Centre in Lakeland, Florida. In real life, Danny was dog dad to a Dachshund called Pepper.

Geronimo & Pico

When singer Bruno Mars first rehomed rescue Rottweiler Geronimo, the first thing he did was apologise in advance to fans for becoming 'that guy', meaning the one who posts endless adoring pictures of his adorable dog. It wasn't too long before Geronimo had his own social-media accounts. After a while, a second rescue, called Pico, joined the Mars clan, with Bruno posting, 'He has no idea how much I love him and all the adventures he and Geronimo will have.' Bruno's hit song 'Marry You' was released on this day in 2011.

23 AUGUST

Lucia

American dancer Gene Kelly apparently loved dogs. So it is fitting that after his death in 1996 his widow, Patricia, got a dog, who she named Lucia, to help her through her grief. Writing some time after Gene's death, she says, 'Gene loved dogs. I wish he and I had one together but the first dog I ever had was a Yellow Lab puppy that I got four years after Gene died. I named her Lucia and she was the best grief therapy. Whenever she found me crying at my desk, she put her paw on my leg and her head in my lap. I don't know how it gets much better than this.' Gene, who was a dancer, singer and actor, was born on this day in 1912. Patricia was his third wife and is a photographer.

24 AUGUST

Fenton

Fenton is a Shetland Sheepdog who has starred in multiple public health campaigns in Scotland, posing for photos in fundraising calendars and taking part in campaigns to promote CPR and even, during the pandemic, to explain the ins and outs of COVID-19. Fenton's owner, Kaylee Garrick, is a paramedic, which explains the link. She was delighted when Fenton's work won him a top award and praise from the judge, the actor Stephen Fry, who was born on this day in 1957.

25 AUGUST

Levi & Pepe

Dog lover and American filmmaker Tim Burton, who celebrates his birthday today, has a Jack Russell Terrier called Levi, but says it was his childhood rescue dog, Pepe, who was the inspiration for the animated dog, Sparky, in his 2012 film, *Frankenweenie*. In the film Victor Frankenstein is a young scientist who creates films starring his dog Sparky, whose name is a reference to the use of electricity in the film. Of course, Sparky is not Tim's only fictional dog; we also have Zero, who stars in *The Nightmare Before Christmas* (1993), and Scraps, who features in *Corpse Bride* (2005). Tim also made the 1991 film *Edward Scissorhands*.

26 AUGUST

Corazon, Whiz & Spark

Pup Academy is a Disney series following the adventures of three dogs: Corazon, a Golden Retriever; Whiz, a Poodle mix; and Spark, a Boxer. The puppies attend the Academy in order to study exactly how to be our best friend, but soon discover a mysterious threat not just to their new academy, but to the very bond between humans and dogs itself. In October 2018, the feature-length pilot and 22 regular episodes were announced by Disney and Netflix, and *Pup Academy* premiered the following year on National Dog Day, which in the USA falls on this day.

27 AUGUST

Mops

Austrian animal painter Carl Reichert, who was born in Vienna on this day in 1836, loved to paint dogs — this was perhaps in his DNA, since he was the son of portrait and animal painter Heinrich Reichert. Carl became particularly well-known for his small-scale, highly detailed dog portraits. *Three Watchful Dogs* is an oil on canvas painting that he painted in 1918. It is now in an anonymous private collection somewhere. Another of his paintings is a portrait of *Mops*, who is clearly the beloved pet of whoever commissioned the piece.

28 AUGUST

Jofi & Wolf

You got two brains for the price of one when you booked a psychoanalysis session with the father of modern analysis, Sigmund Freud, because as often as not his pet Chow Chow would be sitting on his knee. Freud was a fan of Chow Chows while his daughter, Anna, who also became a psychoanalyst, had a German Shepherd called Wolf. Jofi was Freud's favourite dog and so patients quickly became used to her quiet presence in the book-lined consulting room at Freud's home while their analysis took place. Freud always claimed he never needed to look at his watch during a session because, just seconds before the end of the allotted 50 minutes, Jofi would get up and yawn. Freud was awarded the Goethe Prize by the city of Frankfurt on this day in 1930 for his work.

29 AUGUST

Darla

Darla, the Bichon Frisé, has an impressive set of acting credentials. Most notably she played Precious in *The Silence of the Lambs*, adapted from the book by the same name, which was published on this day in 1998. The chilling film, starring Anthony Hopkins and Jodie Foster, scooped four of the Big Five Oscar awards – Best Actor, Best Actress, Best Director and Best Picture – as well as Best Adapted Screenplay at the Academy Awards in 1991. But Daral also featured in many other well-known films, including Tim Burton's 1992 *Batman Returns*, where she played Ratty Poodle, the pet dog of Poodle Lady, whom she helps commit various crimes while working for the Penguin.

Nova

When Rishi Sunak became the UK's 57th Prime Minister, a new dog, Nova, became the top dog in politics. The Red Fox Labrador was rehomed by the family when Rishi was Chancellor of the Exchequer. But on 25 October 2022, he accepted King Charles III's invitation to form a government and was sworn in with an oath he made on the Bhagavad Gita. The Gita is a holy book for Rishi, a devout Hindu, who married his heiress wife, Akshata Murthy, in a simple and low-key traditional ceremony in Bangalore on this day in 2009.

Stoney

Rapper Logic, who celebrates his birthday today (and whose real name is Sir Robert Bryson Hall II), has an Australian Shepherd called Stoney. Growing up in Gaithersburg, Logic built a cult following after the release of his first mixtape, which was called *Young, Broke & Infamous.* He has described himself as a nerdy rapper whose main mantra is peace, love and positivity, and points out his party trick is to rap while solving a Rubik's Cube puzzle. After their divorce in 2018, his ex-wife, Jessica Andrea, kept the couple's two Corgis, who were called Fry and Panda and who often appeared on Logic's YouTube channel.

SEPTEMBER

Smoky

Smoky the Yorkie was a veteran of the Second World War, which began on this day in 1939. The little Terrier was tiny, apparently weighing just 1.8 kg (4 lb) and standing just 18 cm (7 inches) tall. Smoky was found by an American soldier in an abandoned foxhole in the New Guinea jungle in February 1944. The GI who found her sold Smoky to Corporal William A. Wynne, after which she became Wynne's faithful companion, going everywhere with him, serving in the South Pacific as part of the 5th Air Force, 26th Photo Reconnaissance Squadron. She flew air/sea rescue and photo reconnaissance missions and survived 150 air raids. Wynne said she even saved his life by warning him of incoming shells. And in her downtime, the little dog entertained the troops with her clever and funny antics.

Elvis & Moon

Singer-songwriter Neil Young wrote the song 'Old King' for his hound dog, Elvis, who spent years travelling with Young on his tour bus. The singer once said that his dog was the only creature to whom he could confide in 'about everything'! Neil married actress Daryl Hannah (who played a mermaid in the film *Splash)* in the summer of 2018 and the couple share two dogs, one of whom is called Moon. On this day in 1993, the 'Harvest Moon' hit maker joined Pearl Jam on stage to play 'Rockin' in the Free World' at the MTV Music Awards.

3 SEPTEMBER

Nancy, Arfur, Conchita, Eddie & Sausage

In 2023, the animal world mourned as much loved animal champion and Battersea ambassador Paul O'Grady passed away. At the time, Paul had five dogs living on the Kent farm he shared with husband, Andre – Nancy, Arfur, Conchita, Eddie and Sausage. Paul's television show, created in conjunction with Battersea, was called *For the Love of Dogs* and first aired on this day in 2012.

4 SEPTEMBER

Uno

On this day in 2014, Uno the rescue Greyhound saved her entire family's lives by waking them all up as a fire broke out in their house in the middle of the night. She was presented with an award for her bravery. The then five-year-old retired racing dog alerted his owner, Clare, to the blaze by barking furiously at 4 a.m. and the mum of three woke just as the fridge freezer was exploding downstairs. She told reporters, 'The smoke alarm wasn't going off and I couldn't smell the fire, as it was confined to the freezer.' Fire crews arrived shortly after the family, along with Uno, left the property in Washington, Tyne and Wear. And hugging Uno after their lucky escape, Clare said: 'The fire investigator told us Uno saved our lives.'

Spike

American comedian Joan Rivers owned a Yorkshire Terrier called Spike, who went everywhere with the sharp-tongued celebrity. So highly did Rivers think of Spike that the logo for her production company – called PGHM (Please God Help Me) Productions – featured an image of Spike in a praying pose with a halo over his head. Joan made no secret of her preference for animals over people. And it seems her deep love of her 'rescues and runts', as she called them, was a long-term passion. 'I live alone, and my dogs are my best friends,' she once said. *The Joan Rivers Show* premiered on this day in 1989.

6 SEPTEMBER

Dutchess, Bonaparte & Bella

Music legend and country star Emmylou Harris has loved dogs since childhood, when she shared her days with a little Cocker Spaniel named Duchess. The award-winning singer-songwriter had thought that once her career took off she wouldn't have a dog, but that changed one day when she met Bonaparte, a big, black, hairy rescue dog who won her heart and spent 10 years touring with her. 'I just said to him, "Hop on the bus" and he did. He was a great travelling dog, whether it was on the bus, backstage or in hotels.' Harris has now spent most of her adult life rehoming dogs and her hit song, 'Big Black Dog' was inspired by a Black Lab mix she rehomed called Bella. The song is on her album *Hard Bargain*. Looking back on a life with dogs, she adds, 'They're a wonderful part of our lives. They make us more human. They make you more engaged and put you in the moment.' Emmylou was awarded the Swedish Polar Prize for Music on this day in 2015.

Frida

Equipped with goggles and protective boots, Frida, along with 14 other specially trained dogs, helped rescuers save lives following the deadly Mexico City earthquakes which struck on this day in 2017. Deployed by the Mexican Navy, Frida, a Labrador Retriever, was able to crawl into tiny spaces rescuers could not reach to search for signs of survivors. Over the course of a seven-year career, she saved 52 lives and was so loved and admired that even the Mexican President, Enrique Peña Nieto, took to Twitter to sing her praises! Frida spent the run-up to her retirement mentoring younger rescue dogs and is now regarded as a symbol of hope in Mexico.

8 SEPTEMBER

Blue

Blue is the name of the 'stuffed toy' puppy star of the interactive kids' TV show *Blue's Clues*, which premiered on Nickelodeon's Nick Jr. channel on this day in 1996. The little blue dog would put her paws on three different clues and Steve or Joe, the presenters and brothers, would have to deduce the clues, with the help of off-screen children, in order to figure out what Blue wanted to do. The show ran for six seasons across 143 episodes and is still beloved of a whole generation of 90s kids.

9 SEPTEMBER

Meatball

Who says film stars need to be people? Comedy actor Adam Sandler's dog, Meatball, is the sole star of *A Day with the Meatball*, a short comedy film directed by Nicholaus Goossen, which follows Meatball's adventures after he's set free to go out for the day and do as he pleases by owner Adam. Sadly, Meatball passed away at the age of four, but his memory lives on with the videos and photos still shared on Adam's fan website. Adam, who celebrates his birthday today, is now dog dad to a new bulldog, called Matzoball.

10 SEPTEMBER

Urian

Urian was the faithful hound of political whizz Cardinal Thomas Wolsey (1473–1530), the former Lord High Chancellor of Great Britain, who served the Tudor King Henry VIII. Described as England's greatest mediaeval cardinal, Wolsey had a brilliant mastery of foreign affairs and has even been called the Other King of Tudor England. Wolsey fell out of favour with the mercurial Henry after failing to persuade the Pope and the Catholic Church to annul his first marriage to Katherine of Aragon so that the lovesick King could legitimately marry his mistress, Anne Boleyn. Wolsey was invested as a cardinal on this day in 1515.

11 SEPTEMBER

Max

Max was the childhood dog and family pet of One Direction
frontman turned Hollywood actor Harry Styles, who loved his pet
so much that, according to his sister, Gemma, he could often be
found curled up in Max's basket with the Border Collie-Lurcher
cross. One Direction had their first-ever chart-topping single
on this day in 2011 with their debut track, 'What Makes You
Beautiful'. The band went on to become the first UK group to have
their debut album – *Up All Night* – reach No. 1 in the US.

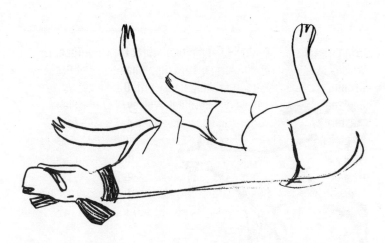

Faunus

Faunus (also called Flush) was a little Cocker Spaniel given to the poet Elizabeth Barrett Browning by her friend and fellow dog lover, Mary Russell Mitford, to relieve the grief Elizabeth felt at the death of her brother in 1840. The dog was mentioned both by Elizabeth and her husband-to-be, Robert Browning, in letters the couple exchanged during their courtship. Elizabeth wrote a poem to the dog, which is called 'To Flush, My Dog' and, on this day in 1846, she eloped with Robert to get married. Most of their courtship had taken place in secret because Elizabeth's strict father did not approve of the younger Robert.

Scooby-Doo

Happy Birthday, Scooby-Doo! The first episode of *Scooby-Doo, Where Are You!* aired on 13 September in 1969. The iconic Great Dane, initially meant to be a large sheepdog, was originally called Too Much but was thankfully renamed by Fred Silverman, the head of programming at CBS, to the unforgettable Scooby-Doo. Scooby-Doo has done it all, working with his best friend Shaggy and the Scooby Gang to solve mysteries in the Mystery Machine. Over the years, Scooby has appeared in several cartoon series, live action films and crossovers with shows such as *Supernatural, Futurama* and *Batman.*

Dusty

Malcolm Turnbull, the former Australian PM, somehow found the time to host a dog blog on his website when he was in office. The three dogs sharing their opinions were Roxy, JoJo and Dusty, the Australian Kelpie. Dog lover Malcolm, who held office from 2015 to 2018, was the leader of the Liberal Party of Australia and a graduate of Oxford University. On this day in 2015, he resigned from the Cabinet and announced he would challenge Tony Abbot's leadership of the party. He won that challenge by 54 votes to 44 in a subsequent leadership ballot and was sworn in as the 29th Prime Minister of the Australia the following day.

15 SEPTEMBER

Einstein & Louis

Before marrying his wife, Amal, and then having twins, film star George Clooney shared his life with two rescue dogs: Cocker Spaniels Einstein and Louis. After marriage, the couple rehomed Millie, a Basset Hound mix. George, who is the nephew of 1950s singer Rosemary Clooney, shot to fame playing the handsome Doctor Ross in the TV series *ER*. He went on to star in major Hollywood films, including the Coen brothers' comedy *O Brother, Where Art Thou?* which was released on this day in 2000.

16 SEPTEMBER

Baby Blue & Zuli

These are the names of the dogs that belong to Marc Anthony – American singer and actor, and former partner of Jennifer Lopez – and his wife, the Paraguayan fashion model Nadia Ferreira. The Pomeranians have almost 50,000 Instagram followers, and rising, and like to pose with their owners, including on their wedding day.

Charlie

Charlie belongs to dog lover and comedian Tim Allen, who in the movie *Shaggy Dog*, plays a workaholic lawyer who takes a strange serum that turns him into a 300-year-old sacred Tibetan Bearded Collie sheepdog called Khyi Yang Po. Tim is best known for playing the television host dad in the hit family comedy *Home Improvement*, which premiered on this day in 1991 and ran for 204 episodes over eight seasons.

Mystery Newfoundland

His name may have been long lost to the history books, but his antics made it onto the pages of the *New York Times* in 1908 when the journalists reported the story of a dog who saved a child who had fallen into the River Seine. The story – or so it goes – is that a Newfoundland quickly jumped into the waters to rescue a struggling child and save the day. And the happy story doesn't end there as, apparently, the dog's heroic antics were rewarded with a nice juicy steak.

Muick & Sandy

Her Majesty Queen Elizabeth II owned over 30 Corgis during her long reign and many dog lovers will have been moved by the sight of two of those dogs, Muick and Sandy, paying tribute to Her Majesty on the day of her funeral. The dogs had been given to The Queen to keep her company during the COVID-19 pandemic and were shown waiting for her casket to pass by on its way to her committal ceremony in Windsor on this day in 2022. For us dog lovers, it was a poignant sight. Her Majesty The Queen became a patron of Battersea in 1956 and paid official visits to the London centre in 1991 and 2015.

Bear & Finnegan

These two rescue dogs belong to actress Mackenzie Hancsicsak, who plays the young Kate Pearson in the hit Amazon Prime show *This Is Us*. Kate explains that her dad had owned a dog called Bear growing up and so she thought it was fitting that the family's rescue dog should have the same name. And Kate's not the only dog lover among the *This Is Us* cast: actress Mandy Moore, who plays mum Rebecca Pearson, has a dog called Jackson; and Chris Sullivan, who plays grown up Kate's husband, Toby Damon, has two dogs, Sally and Harrison.

21 SEPTEMBER

Pluto

Disney cartoon dog Pluto is a yellow-orange, short-haired dog with black ears who is named after one of the two planets that the English composer Gustav Holst did not include in his best-known work, *The Planets.* (If you are a *Star Wars* fan, then you'll know the track called 'Mars, the bringer of War)'. Although Bloodhound Pluto was originally Minnie Mouse's dog (and originally called Rover), his name was changed to Pluto and his owner switched to Mickey Mouse, and he became one of the best-known Disney dogs of all time. Holst, who died on this day in 1874, did not include the planet Pluto in his composition because the planet was not discovered until 1930.

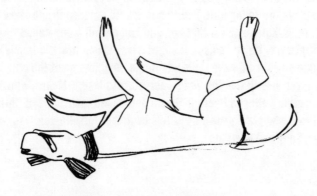

22 SEPTEMBER

Splash

Although he's best known for playing the suave ad agency creative director Don Draper in the HBO hit series *Mad Men*, Jon Hamm, who is a rescue advocate and owner of Splash, made his film debut with just one line in the Clint Eastwood film *Space Cowboys*, which was released on this day in 2000. Splash has now happily found his forever home with Jon and is currently living his best puppy life. Jon had originally planned to just foster Splash but says the dog brought so much 'pure joy and love into his life' he soon made the arrangement a permanent one.

Pippin & Mr Higgins

Come Outside was a British educational kids' show which ran from September 1993 to March 1997. It was presented by and starred Lynda Baron as Auntie Mabel and her dog, Pippin, who was played by a dog called... Pippin. (And then, in later seasons, by Pippin's real-life grandson, who was called Mr Higgins.) Pippin would often get up to mischief without Mabel knowing. For example, in the episode 'A Carton Drink', she eats the sausages from her lunchbox; in the episode 'Soap', she hides the bar of soap to avoid having a bath; and the episode 'A Woolly Jumper' ends with Pippin finding a jumper knitted by Auntie Mabel, and then pulling on it and causing it to unravel. The idea of the show, which was so popular that it was reprised by CBeebies and repeated on that channel until 2012, was to teach young children about the world around them.

24 SEPTEMBER

Benji

Dog actor Benji was so successful he was known as the 'Laurence Olivier of the dog world'. He was the star of multiple films, including *Benji, For the Love of Benji* and *Oh! Heavenly Dog*, as well as television shows, and was in so much demand he even attended his own press interviews at the 1978 Cannes Film Festival. Benji, whose real name was Higgin, was a Cocker Spaniel, Schnauzer and Poodle mix who was owned by the Hollywood animal trainer Frank Inn. He made his screen debut in the film *Petticoat Junction* in 1963.

25 SEPTEMBER

Mr Sniff

On this day in 1968, the Welsh songbird Mary Hopkin, who also recorded 'The Puppy Song', was at No. 1 in the UK singles chart with her hit 'Those Were the Days'. Mary had signed to the Beatles' Apple label after appearing on the UK TV talent show *Opportunity Knocks*, which was hosted by larger-than-life presenter Hughie Green. Host Hughie was the father of Paula Yates, whose daughter, Pixie Geldof, completed the family canine connection by owning a long-haired Chihuahua, called Mr Sniff.

Rufus & Rufus II

Sir Winston Churchill had two great dog loves, both miniature brown Poodles and both named Rufus. And while the second Rufus was called Rufus II, Churchill would tell people with his trademark wit, 'but the II is silent'. The Churchill family tell the story of how, when relaxing in front the TV at Chequers one weekend and watching one dramatic scene in the film of *Oliver Twist*, Churchill covered the poodle's eyes and said, 'Don't look now, I'll tell you about it afterwards.' Rufus II, who was said to have 'breath like a flamethrower', ate with the family in the dining room, seated on a Persian rug and served by a butler. The film *Oliver!* – a later musical adaptation of the story – was released on this day in 1968.

Neville Jacobs

Dog, author and social media superstar Neville Jacobs has been living the life of an international jet setter with his human companion, fashion designer Marc Jacobs, for years. Dubbed 'the hardest working dog in fashion' by *T Magazine*, Neville Jacobs is a sweet-natured Bull Terrier who, thanks to his activity on Instagram, has become just as popular as his owner. When he's not travelling the globe, Neville lives in New York. An esteemed author, his first book, an autobiography called *Neville Jacobs: I'm Marc's Dog*, was published on this day in 2016.

Tinkles

Cartoon dog Tinkles is Dennis's pet Pug puppy from the *Hotel Transylvania* short called, simply, *Puppy!* Toots is Tinkles' love interest in the films and on his official fandom page we learn he likes eating bones and skeletons, playing with Dennis and 'meat drooling'. Tinkles is huge, has black fur, wide eyes with large black pupils, a red collar and a red, yellow, blue and white ball. He tends to jump a lot when he gets excited and becomes super obedient when bribed with meat. The longer film, *Hotel Transylvania*, which also features Tinkles, was released on this day in 2012.

29 SEPTEMBER

Huckleberry Hound

Huckleberry Hound is a cartoon dog that speaks in a slow Tennessee drawl. He first appeared in the Emmy-winning show *The Huckleberry Hound Show,* which first aired on this day in 1958. The affable blue-skinned canine calmly overcame all the obstacles in his path as he tried on a number of different careers, including cowboy, chef, lion tamer, police officer, farmer and, as Huckleberry himself would say, 'stuff like that there'. The show was the launch pad for another huge cartoon character hit, Yogi Bear.

30 SEPTEMBER

Sausage Dog

Singer-songwriter Yusuf/Cat Stevens wrote arguably the best dog song ever when he penned 'I Love My Dog'. The song was all about a Dachshund which he'd found apparently abandoned outside Foyles bookshop in London when he was young. Cat took the sausage dog home and, since nobody ever claimed it, kept it. He was just 17 when he wrote this song, which tells a lady love that, while she may not last, his love for his dog will. The song, which was his first single and the one that earned him a record deal, was released on this day in 1966.

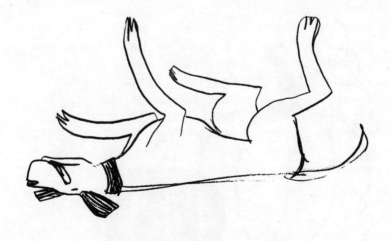

OCTOBER

1 OCTOBER

Daisy

Spice Girl Geri Horner (formerly Halliwell) rehomed Daisy from Battersea in 2021. Dog lover Geri had rehomed from Battersea before – her constant companion on the red carpet and at showbiz events at one time was Harry, also a Shih Tzu mix, found with the help of her friend, the late Wham! singer, George Michael. Introducing Daisy to fans on her Instagram pages, Geri wrote, 'Meet Daisy! She's a rescue dog from @battersea that needed a second chance in love and a family... And Daisy is a mix of shih-tzu, just like Harry (who was also from @battersea too.)' On this day in 2007, the Spice Girl London Reunion concert sold out in 38 seconds after tickets went on sale.

2 OCTOBER

Dot & Zelda

It was love at first sight for American actor and musician Zooey Deschanel and shelter dog Dot – and when big-hearted Zooey heard that Dot had a sister called Zelda, she offered her a home too so that the sisters would not be parted, describing her canine companions as 'the greatest, sweetest most wonderful dogs in the world. Apples of my eye.' Supporting the 'Adopt, Don't Shop!' slogan, Zooey encourages others to share photos of their rescue dogs on their social media channels, adding that rehoming was a no-brainer for her because 'I wanted something cute to hang out with and hug.' As we celebrate the whole ethos behind rescuing animals, we celebrate the founding of Battersea on this day in 1860.

3 OCTOBER

Swansea Jack

This famous Welsh dog was a black flat-coated Retriever who saved 27 people from drowning in the North Dock and River Tawe areas of Swansea between 1931 and 1937. Known locally as 'Swansea Jack' or 'Newfoundland dog' (he is believed to have been born in Newfoundland), Jack lived in the area with owner William Thomas and was soon known as a four-legged guardian angel for that part of Swansea – keeping an ear out for cries of help from the water. Jack was given a 'Dog of the Century' award and, on this day in 2021, a festival was held in Wales in Jack's honour.

4 OCTOBER 4

Snoopy, Bell, Marbles, Andy, Olaf, Molly & Rover

You'll find this crew of dog siblings in the Charlie Brown *Peanuts* comic strips and the animated films based on them, because this is Snoopy's four-legged dog family. You might describe Snoopy himself as 'the clever one' and it's clear he's no ordinary Beagle. According to his fan page, he is a book lover – he reads *War and Peace* at the rate of a word a day – a book writer, a collector of fine art and a root beer connoisseur. And his unstoppable imagination helps keep his life anything but ordinary. As the Flying Ace, he heroically battles the Red Baron. As Joe Cool, he is the big dog on campus. Snoopy made his first appearance on this day in 1950.

5 OCTOBER

Lila

At the Battle of Germantown, which took place in 1777 as part of the American Revolution, British forces in Pennsylvania defeated the American Continental Army under the command of General George Washington. Lila, a dog belonging to the British Commander in Chief, Sir Willliam Howe, somehow wandered off and was recovered by American troops who fed her, cleaned her up and the following day (5 October) brought her back to the British camp under the flag of truce. The little dog was returned along with a cordial note from General Washington.

6 OCTOBER

Doc

Actor Ellen Pomeo – also known as Dr Meredith Grey in the hit TV series *Grey's Anatomy* – is a huge dog lover, so it was no surprise when one storyline featured her heading to the dog shelter to rehome a dog she called Doc. The mixed-breed dog, likely a Briard mix, appeared in Seasons 2, 3 and 15 of the show and was a firm fan favourite. Meredith rehomed him after her crush, Derek, returned to an old flame and so we first saw Doc, who cheered her up, in an episode entitled 'Owner of a Lonely Heart'. The 19th season of *Grey's Anatomy* premiered in the US on this day in 2022.

7 OCTOBER

Duke

Rescue dog Duke hit the headlines when he saved the life of a nine-week-old baby by waking his owners, the Brousseau family, in the middle of the night by jumping on the bed and shaking uncontrollably – both behaviours that his owners knew to be out of character for the dog they had rehomed six years before. Somehow, a magical and lifesaving wordless communication between the dog and its humans worked and the couple checked on baby Harper, who had stopped breathing. The couple called 911 and the paramedics arrived in time to revive the little girl, who was taken to hospital to be checked but who was subsequently found to be as right as rain.

Wishbone

Wishbone is the star of an award-winning children's show in which a little Jack Russell Terrier who lives with his owner, Joe Talbot, in the fictional town of Oakdale, daydreams about being the lead character in famous stories from classic literature. He was known as 'the little dog with a big imagination'. Only the viewers and the characters in his daydreams can hear Wishbone speak, with the latter only able to see him as whichever famous character he is currently portraying and not as a dog. Originally shown on US channel PBS and later shown in the UK on Nickelodeon, the 50-episode show first aired on this day in 1995.

Dug & Alpha

Dug is the Golden Retriever who can talk in the animated Pixar film *Up*. He is the misfit of a pack of dogs, led by talking Doberman Pinscher Alpha. The two dogs have the ability to talk thanks to their electrical collars, which translate their thoughts to words. When Dug first meets his new owner, his unabashed first words are, 'I have just met you, and I love you.' Alpha is a little tougher and, according to creator Pete Docter, thinks of himself as more of a Clint Eastwood figure. Unfortunately, instead of speaking in an intimidating bass voice, Alpha's collar has a malfunction, which means he speaks in a high-pitched, squeaky voice, as if he has inhaled helium. The film was released in the UK on this day in 2009.

10 OCTOBER

Fifi & Morningstar

Morningstar was a little white Poodle who belonged to the Hollywood actor Natalie Woods. The little poodle was named after Natalie's character in the 1958 romance film *Marjorie Morningstar*. She also had a silver Poodle called Fifi and liked to include both her dogs in her glamorous photoshoots. Natalie, who had successfully made the sometimes difficult transition from child actor to adult, won a Best Newcomer Golden Globe for her role opposite James Dean in *Rebel Without a Cause*, and later starred alongside Warren Beatty in the period drama *Splendor in the Grass*, which was released on this day in 1961.

Pat

When Pat – an Irish Terrier owned by the former Canadian Prime Minister William Lyon Mackenzie King – passed away, his distraught owner held séances to try to communicate with the dog. As Prime Minster of Canada, King was appointed to the Privy Council of the United Kingdom in 1922 and subsequently sworn in at Buckingham Palace on this day a year later. Canada's tenth and longest serving Prime Minister, bachelor King was a devoted dog lover his whole life. Pat was the first of his Terriers and he would chronicle his adventures in his daily diaries, describing him as 'a God-sent little angel in the guise of a dog, my dear little saviour'.

BeeGee

We can only hope that rock star dogs are better behaved than their famously raucous owners, because lots of musicians seem to be dog owners. One such example is Foo Fighters frontman and former Nirvana drummer Dave Grohl, who has spoken of his family dog, BeeGee, named after his favourite disco group. Grohl tells the story of how his cousins' dog had puppies, and his family couldn't resist taking one home, where it stayed with them for a 16 happy years. Dave's band Nirvana hit the big time with their record *Nevermind*, which was certified gold on this day in 1991.

Rocks & Daphne

In the family sequel *Look Who's Talking Now*, the chaos and comedy ante is upped with the arrival of dogs who, just like baby Mikey in the original film, can talk too. Rocks is a street dog voiced by Danny DeVito and Daphne is a glamorous but spoiled Poodle played by Diane Keaton. And, of course, the two dogs do not hit it off at first and comedy ensues. The original film, *Look Who's Talking*, was released on this day in 1993.

Smokey

Another supporter of rehoming dogs is *The Real Housewives of Beverly Hills* (RHOBH) star Kyle Richards, who added a little dog called Smokey to her dog clan, which already included Storm, Bambi, Romeo, Luna and River. Introducing Smokey to fans via her Instagram account, the actor and producer wrote, 'When we heard Smokey needed a home my heart stopped.' *RHOBH* premiered on Bravo on this day in 2010 with Kyle (and her dogs) an original cast member.

15 OCTOBER

Naki'o

Brave Naki'o, who lost all four paws and his tail due to frostbite
when he was a puppy, became the first dog to have four prosthetic
'bionic paws' made. The mixed-breed dog had a tough start to life
and had been left abandoned at a foreclosed Nebraska home when
he was a young. After being discovered, he was taken to an animal
rescue centre, and under their care his injured paws healed to
rounded stumps. After having his bionic paws fitted, Naki'o went on
to star as the hero in his own storybook when his adopter, Christie,
wrote a children's book called *Stubby and his Magic Boots*. The
book, based on the life of Naki'o, was published on this day in 2015.

Petra

Blue Peter's very first dog, Petra, made her studio debut in 1962 but apparently didn't much like the television set and was really only happy once presenter Peter Purves joined and claimed her as his companion, after which she settled down. Now immortalised as the nation's favourite pet with a statue in the *Blue Peter* garden, Petra was a Rough Collie cross who was on the show until 1977. These were the days when dogs were put on display in shop windows for sale, and so when the TV producers spotted the small browny-black puppy looking forlorn in a shop window in Lewisham, they snapped her up and asked viewers to choose her name. The popular children's show first aired on this day in 1958.

Bamse

Brave Bamse – prounounced *bump-sa*, which is the Norwegian word for 'teddy bear' – was a St Bernard who became the heroic mascot of the Free Norwegian Forces during the Second World War. In fact, the sea dog has a life-size statue to his memory, which was made by Scottish sculptor Alan Herriot and unveiled on this day in 2006 in the Scottish town of Montrose. Bamse was owned by the Hafto family, who lived in the small Norwegian town of Honningsvag. But Bamse was stationed in Tayside during the war and it was there that he saved the lives of two Norwegian sailors. Further tales of his adventures, courage and kindness soon spread and when he died in 1944, the 89-kg (14-stone) dog was buried with full military honours.

Marley

John Grogan, the writer of the book that was adapted for the hit film *Marley & Me*, has no doubt we can learn a lot from dogs. Towards the end of the book, he writes about how dogs love unconditionally and love you, flaws and all: 'Animals aren't concerned with social class or status, they're much more pure, heart to heart. A dog can teach us what matters most in life and what's important in life if we open our heart and listen.' John's book was published on this day in 2005.

Elf's Dog

Have you woken up on the wrong side of bed? Not really feeling it today? Well, fear not, for it's well known among dog lovers that any bad day can immediately be improved by spotting a great dog. It's a fact that was immortalised in the much-loved Christmas movie *Elf*, starring Will Ferrell and directed by Jon Favreau, who enjoys his birthday today. As Buddy, a Christmas elf who finds himself in New York City, walks with his new friend he utters the wonderful conversation starter, 'So, good news – I saw a dog today.' Sadly he doesn't go on to share any further information about the encounter, but any as admirer of our four-legged friends will agree, it's cause for celebration.

20 OCTOBER

Sansa & Arya

These two Red Fox Labradors are owned by TV presenter Jeremy Clarkson and named after the Stark sisters in the *Game of Thrones* hit series. In the drama, all the Stark siblings were given a Direwolf — sigil of House Stark — which were said to belong to the wolf family. Intelligent, fierce and loyal, Sansa named hers Lady, while Arya called hers Nymeria, afer Nymeria of Dorne, the warrior-queen of the Rhoynar who (in the book series *A Song of Ice and Fire*) lived 1,000 years ago. Jeremy Clarkson made his name on TV presenting the BBC's motoring show *Top Gear*, the revived, modern version of which premiered on this day in 2002.

21 OCTOBER

Charley

Charley went on the road with his owner, the writer John Steinbeck, and ended up as the main star of a book that even carried his name. *Travels with Charley: In Search of America* chronicles the 1960 road trip the duo made together, with Steinbeck explaining that, since he earned his living writing about America, he thought it a good idea to try to see some more of it. Charley was a Standard Poodle and may well have been the inspiration behind one of Steinbeck's better-known quotes: 'I am convinced that basically dogs think humans are nuts.' The book bearing Charley's name reached the top of the *New York Times* Best Sellers list on this day in 1962.

Todd

Todd was the very first winner of the inaugural Dog Of the Year Honor presented by the Streamy Awards, which recognises great content from the world's top online video creators. The story of Todd, who saved his owner from a rattlesnake, went viral and he was voted Dog of the Year by fans on social media site Twitter. Todd received his award on this day in 2018 from noted dog lover and Olympic medallist Gus Kenworthy. The awards founder, Drew Baldwin, said dogs are still the internet's favourite animals and added, 'The world wouldn't be the same without dogs; lives are often transformed because of them, and it's time that we honor all the joy that they give to us.'

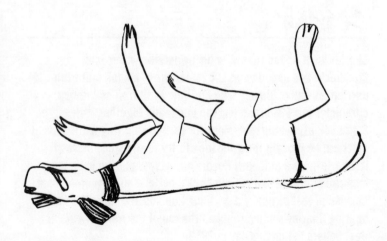

23 OCTOBER

Jump & Trashcan

Jump is a smart dog who is fiercely loyal and receptive to commands, but he has a mind of his own and won't do tricks which he thinks are beneath him. We meet Jump in the animated film *Astro Boy*, which was released on this day in 2009 and which is loosely based on Osamu Tezuka's manga series of the same name. The film follows an android replica of a boy who goes off on adventures to find his own identity. Jump is a beige Australian Terrier, though the film also features Trashcan, a robot dog of above average intelligence who was originally destined to be a garbage bin that could move on its own but who was instead programmed to be a domestic dog.

24 OCTOBER

Duke

As a little boy, the film star John Wayne – whose real name was Marion Robert Morrison – went everywhere with the family dog, an Airedale terrier named Duke. And, of course, once he was famous, Wayne himself was known as The Duke. Wayne's first starring role came in 1930 with a film called *The Big Trail*, which was directed by Raoul Walsh. It was Raoul who suggested John change his name because he thought Marion was not a good name for an actor playing a tough Western hero. That film was released on this day in 1930.

25 OCTOBER

Lump

Artist Pablo Picasso produced many continuous-line drawings of animals, and his dachshund, Lump, was the inspiration for many of them. Picasso, who was born on this day in 1881, owned many breeds of dogs over the years – including Terriers, Poodles, Afghan Hounds, a German Shepherd, a Boxer and a Great Pyrenees – but the 'dog love of his life' was Lump. The artist himself said it was more like a love affair than anything else and Lump appeared in many of his paintings.

26 OCTOBER

Bouncer

Bouncer is the Labrador Retriever who won the hearts of millions of fans when he spent six years starring in the Australian daytime soap *Neighbours*, which chronicled the lives and loves of the residents of fictional Ramsey Street. Bouncer apparently received more fan cards than anyone else on the show and one of his most memorable storylines was when he dreamt he was marrying Rosie, the Border Collie who lived next door. *Neighbours* was first aired in the UK on October 26 1986.

27 OCTOBER

Floki

Floki is a Shiba Inu dog who inspired a cryptocurrency called Dogecoin. His owner is, not surprisingly, billionaire Tesla majority shareholder and now Twitter owner Elon Musk, who took over the global social media platform on this day in 2022, paying $44 billion for the deal. The Shiuba Inu is a little known and well-muscled Japanese breed. Today, this good-natured dog is the most popular companion dog in Japan.

28 OCTOBER

Oreo & Nilla

Microsoft founder turned philanthropist Bill Gates has two family dogs, Oreo and Nilla, who is a Poodle mix. The Poodle is believed to have originated in Germany, with its name coming from the German word *pudelin*, meaning 'to splash'. Bill Gates, who is worth an estimated $110.7 billion – making him the fourth richest person in the world – will be celebrating his birthday today.

29 OCTOBER

Jackson P

Jackson 'Jack' P was a Jack Russell Terrier and singer Mariah's Carey's first dog. In one interview, when the singing superstar was just starting out on her career, she told *K9 Magazine* the amazing little white Terrier could swim under water and jump four feet in the air. Mariah also said the playful dog was forever like a puppy, even in maturity. On this day in 1994, Mariah released the Christmas hit 'All I Want For Christmas Is You', which she co-wrote with Walter Afanasieff. It became one of her biggest all-time hits across the world and in 2019 it reached No. 1 on the Billboard Hot 100 charts – 25 years after it was first released.

30 OCTOBER

Charlie & Griz

Charlie and Griz belong to the Yawi family – also known as the Tannerites – a family of nine who chronicle their ups and downs on their award-winning video channel and vlogs. The family makes kid-friendly videos showing how life can be all about making memories, building relationships (including with our pets) and learning to love. We're sure there will be plenty more memories made in the Yawi family household today because it is third child Savannah's birthday today.

Jade

Jade is the German Shepherd who saved a newborn baby's life after finding the tiny infant hidden in bushes in the Birmingham park where Jade's owner, Roger Wilday, was walking her. 'Jade headed to the bushes and wouldn't come back, so I had to go over and I saw a toy shop bag and then I heard a baby cry. I reached down to look at the bag closer and I saw a baby in a blue blanket, I was so shocked. I dialled 999 and picked the baby up. She was a tiny thing. She was warm, so I don't think she had been there long,' Roger told reporters. The baby, who was found on this day in 2013, was taken straight to hospital and cared for. And proud dog dad, Roger, went on to explain that Jade has grown up with children around her. 'She loves babies and she's a hero.'

NOVEMBER

1 NOVEMBER

Arthur

This is the day that entries for the Adventure World Racing championships open for those who wish to take part in the gruelling endurance race. For fans of the globe-trotting series, the story of Arthur is an uplifting one. Arthur was an Ecuadorian stray who demonstrated his own brand of endurance in 2014, when he attached himself to a team and followed them 160 km (100 miles) across jungle terrain to the finishing line. Arthur was so inspiring that one member of the team, Mikael Lindnor, turned his story into a book, which was published two years later. In the book, he describes how the stoical Arthur became his dog and his best friend.

2 NOVEMBER

Kabosu

This Shiba Inu was rehomed in 2008 by Japanese teacher Atsuko Sato, and named after the citrus fruit kabosu because Sato thought she had a round face like the fruit. Kabosu, who was born on this day in 2005, went on to become the famous face behind the viral 'Doge' meme which became popular in 2013. The meme was based on a 2010 photograph and later named as Know Your Meme's 'top meme' of 2013. The Shiba Inu breed made its mark in popular culture in late 2013 with a new cryptocurrency based on Doge – the Dogecoin – launching in December of that year. Several online polls and media outlets recognised Doge as one of the most popular internet memes of the 2010s.

3 NOVEMBER

Laika

'Dog Star' is a 1962 science fiction short story by the British writer Arthur C. Clarke. It tells the story of an astronomer living on a moon base, who awakes from a dream in which his dog, Laika, is barking. Too scared to fall back asleep, he remembers how the dog, which he had rescued after finding her on the side of the road, had saved his life once before when she alerted him to an impending earthquake when he was still on Earth.

Digby

Max Woosey, who became known as the Boy in the Tent, spent three whole years sleeping in a tent outside to raise money for the North Devon hospice that had helped care for a tragically ill family friend. Max raised a staggering £700,000 for his efforts but he was not alone and, when the TV cameras came calling to talk to Max on the last night of sleeping outside, it was the family dog, Digby, who stole the limelight, barking every time Max was asked a question. When Max travelled to London on his 12th birthday in October 2021 to receive a prestigious Pride of Britain award, he slept on the hotel balcony. Viewers saw Max, who has now set a Guinness World Record, receive his award when the televised event was aired on ITV on this day the following month.

Louie, Dora, Rosy & Snowball

The actor Tilda Swinton, who celebrates her birthday today, once made her dogs the stars of an operatic music video. The video shows Tilda's four Springer Spaniels running around to the sound of the operatic masterpiece 'Rompo I lacci' (which translates to 'I break the laces'), originally written by Handel for the famous *castrato* Senesino. The video, which shows Louie, Dora, Rosy and Snowball all swimming and jumping to fetch a ball, was made for Opera Philadelphia's Glass Handel project.

Bulldog Jack

Having survived an explosion in the Bond film, *Skyfall*, Jack the Bulldog makes a reappearance in the following film *Spectre*, which was released on this day in 2015. You may have spotted Jack, a Royal Doulton figure, in pride of place on M's desk. And you perhaps noticed that Bond himself seemed a little less than enthused when he learned M would bequeath the statue to him.

Ru

He's rubbed noses with the world's top fashionistas because Boston Terrier Ru – named after the Boston drag artist RuPaul – belongs to British *Vogue* editor-in-chief Edward Enninful. In 1930, the magazine declared, 'The next best thing to having the world at your feet is to have a dog at your heels', so it's no surprise that multiple *Vogue* editors, stylists and photographer have chosen to put dogs on their covers alongside the world's top supermodels. On this day in 1665, *The London Gazette,* which is the world's oldest surviving journal, was first published.

8 NOVEMBER

Peanut, Carlos, Bruno & Truffle

He may not be a fan of incompetence in the kitchen but shouty chef Gordon Ramsey is a huge dog lover and these four belong to him and wife Tana. Gordon's pets regularly pop up on his social media accounts and he is such a fan of four-legged family members that he has even made his London Battersea, Chelsea and Camden and Limehouse restaurants dog-friendly, making sure water for the dog(s) is brought to the table when they arrive. Today is daughter Matilda (Tilly) Ramsey's birthday. Tilly is also a chef and dog lover.

9 NOVEMBER

Patti & Peggy

Patti the Poochon belongs to the actor, comedienne and TV writer Miranda Hart, whose 2016 bestselling memoir was called *Peggy and Me* (with Peggy being the Shih Tzu-Bichon Frisé cross that has been Miranda's constant companion since she arrived in 2007). New dog Patti's full name, says Miranda, is Dame Patience Pattercake Hart the Poochon of Portsmouth! Miranda's smash hit TV show, simply called *Miranda,* premiered on this day in 2009.

10 NOVEMBER

Mike

There may not be many Great Danes called Mike and there are certainly no other Great Danes who once wore one of the world's most fabulous and sought-after diamonds on the collar around their neck. But Mike was no ordinary Great Dane. He was the pampered pooch of Ned and Evalyn Walsh McLean, a young couple who were the toast of Washington's social circles in the early 1900s. The couple, both the only children of wealthy families, had been on honeymoon in Paris when they swung by the Cartier store and were shown the blue Hope Diamond, which they purchased for $300,000 (about $6.2 million today). Cartier had set the stone into a headpiece, but Evalyn wanted it put back to a traditional necklace, which she was rarely seen without, and liked to decorate Mike's collar with it for parties. The Hope Diamond is now on display at the National Museum of Natural History in Washington.

11 NOVEMBER

Mina, Marco & Meg

The English composer Sir Edward Elgar loved his dogs and named his final orchestral work after his Cairn Terrier, Mina. After 30 years of not being able to have a dog because his wife, Alice, forbade them in the house, that changed when she passed away and he got three all at once – Marco, a Spaniel, and two Terriers, Meg and Mina. Elgar's dogs were always at his side and, even when apart, he would talk to them. On his 70th birthday, he stopped mid-flow during a live radio broadcast to wish his dogs goodnight and, while dining in a fancy London club, once took an urgent telephone call and was heard by his fellow diners to tell someone to stop biting the cushions. Elgar's 'Nimrod' is always played on Remembrance Day to honour the fallen.

12 NOVEMBER

Bug, Baby & Kitty

Bug and Bay are two miniature Dobermans belonging to American singer-songwriter Taylor Swift, who grew up with dogs. Taylor, an animal lover and advocate, made the bold move on this day in 2014 to pull her entire back catalogue of music from the streaming service Spotify. She makes no secret of her great love of animals, but Kitty actually belongs to her mom Andrea, who apparently rehomed the Great Dane to keep her company when her daughter is away on tour.

13 NOVEMBER

Rags

Scene-stealing Rags (real name Bolt) is the St Bernard-Australian Shepherd mix who joins the Cooper family for their Christmas get-together in the festive holiday film *Love the Coopers*. The whole film is, in fact, narrated by Rags, voiced by comedian Steve Martin. Despite a stellar cast, it was Bolt who really shone, with director Jesse Nelson claiming, 'He's the Marlon Brando of dogs!' *Love the Coopers* was released on this day in 2015.

14 NOVEMBER

Flyer & Scipio

Orville and Wilbur Wright – the famous American aviation pioneers who made the world's first powered flight in 1903 – absolutely loved dogs, and while neither had time to date or marry, they did find time for their four-legged family members. In 1908, the brothers were finally ready to show the world their flying machine. They built two planes, and Orville planned to take one to show the US Army while Wilbur took the other to France to show the public. Wilbur's plane was damaged when it got to France, so he had to spend days in a shed rebuilding it. While there, a stray dog approached and the two became friends. Wilbur rehomed the dog and named him Flyer. Orville later met up with Wilbur, and for the next year the brothers and Flyer would travel Europe showing off their plane. Later in life, Orville bought a St Bernard puppy. His sister named the dog Scipio, after the Roman general who is best known for defeating Hannibal at the Battle of Zama in 202 BC. On this date, the Wright Brothers National Memorial (in North Carolina) was dedicated in 1932.

Polaris

Polaris is a black German Shepherd who was abandoned at San Francisco International Airport. Customer services swung into action to get the dog the correct entry papers and, by the time he was 'legal', over 30 members of the company had applied to rehome the dog, who was named after both the North Star and the airline's business lounge at the airport. And when Polaris joined the family of United pilot Captain William Dale, the company threw a rehoming party for the dog and his new family. The British-German astronomer who first found the North Star, William Herschel, was born on this day in 1738.

Hugo

Fang is Groundskeeper Hagrid's dog in the much-loved books and films of the Harry Potter series. In the books, Fang is a Boarhound, which is an old term for a Great Dane, while in the films, he is a Neapolitan Mastiff. Fang was played in the first three Harry Potter films by a dog called Hugo, who had been rehomed from an animal shelter in Northampton by top animal trainer Julie Tottman. Julie worked as Harry Potter's head animal trainer between 2000 and 2011 and trained more than 250 animals for the films, including owls, cats and even spiders! The first *Harry Potter* film came out on this day in 2001.

17 NOVEMBER

Terry

Canine actor Terry – most famously known for playing Toto in
The Wizard of Oz – was born on this day in 1933. She was paid
$125 a week (equivalent to around $2,400 now) to star as Toto.
Terry was a Cairn Terrier rehomed at the age of one by Carl Spitz,
ex-military dog trainer and owner of the Hollywood Dog Training
School. After attending a casting call for a dog resembling
Dorothy's in the *The Wizard of Oz* books, Terry immediately bonded
with star Judy Garland and was hired. She lived with Garland for
two weeks – the star apparently offered to rehome her, but Spitz
refused. Over her acting career, Terry made a total of 23 film
appearances, though *The Wizard of Oz* was her only credited role.

18 NOVEMBER

Rex

Rex likes to play and bury things. He is an animated dog, voiced
by Jim Cummings, who we meet in the Disney Junior series *Sofia
the First*. Rex is a bit goofy but actually smarter than he lets on,
except when he buries an important spell book and promptly
forgets which hole he dug for it. He is a Foxhound who belongs
to Sofia's older brother, Prince James, and lives in the magical
kingdom of Enchancia with his family. *Sofia the First* was first
aired on this day in 2012.

19 NOVEMBER

Adie, Dutch & Sippie

Award-winning actor Allison Janney, who celebrates her birthday today, says she gains her 'zen' through walking her three dogs, Adie, Dutch and Sippie. The dogs are all Australian Cattle Dog mixes and Allison says she makes sure her day starts and ends on a positive note by walking the trio. 'My dogs are my positivity role models, they really are,' she says. 'Dogs love regardless of accolades, size of a paycheck or good hair day. All three are rescues and I'm so grateful I adopted them. Animals are a game-changer for our spirits and our souls.' Alison played the President's smart-talking press secretary C.J. in the hit series *The West Wing*.

20 NOVEMBER

Bodger & Luath

Ageing Bull Terrier Bodger and lively Labrador Retriever Luath are the dog stars of a film called *The Incredible Journey*, which was released on this day in 1963. The duo team up with a Siamese cat called Tao to make their way back home after being dropped off for the summer to stay with a family friend who lives 400 km (250 miles) away. The Disney film was directed by Fletcher Markle and tells the story of how the plucky trio face challenge after challenge to get back to the family they love.

21 NOVEMBER

Sox & Baxter

Blur band member turned farmer Alex James will probably celebrate his birthday today with some artisan cheese and cider, as that's what he makes on his Cotswolds farm. Dog lover Alex once posed with his Whippet, Sox, for animal portrait photographer Gerrard Gethings in an exhibition called *The Company of Dogs*. Gerrard aims to capture the likeness between people and their dogs and is assisted in his work on 'dogglegangers' by his own look-a-like Border Terrier assistant, Baxter.

22 NOVEMBER

Cutty Sark Collies

One of England's most famous sea captains was Norfolk-born Richard Woodget, who also happened to be a breeder of Collie dogs, some of whom travelled with him to Australia aboard his most famous command, the *Cutty Sark*, which he sailed from 1885 to 1895. Captain Woodget made 10 voyages to Australia, several of which broke new records and all of which were faster than any other ship on the Australian wool trade route. The descendants of the Collie dogs he took with him were soon making headlines in the Australian show rings. The *Cutty Sark* was a Scottish clipper, which was launched from Dumbarton on this day in 1869. Under the dog-loving captain's command, the ship, which is now a tourist attraction in London's Greenwich, was used to bring wool from Australia back to England.

23 NOVEMBER

Mate

Singer Miley Cyrus named her German Shepherd after her all-time favourite Australian word, which is 'mate'. Miley's Instagram is proof enough that she loves nothing more than a cuddle with her dogs. In 2012, she and her ex-partner Liam Hemsworth rehomed a Rottweiler-Beagle mix and since then she has had multiple dogs (and cats, a pig and even a blowfish!). Today is Miley's birthday.

24 NOVEMBER

Polly & Bob

We know the great scientist Charles Darwin loved dogs because he talked about them in his writings. One of his dogs was Polly, a rough white Fox Terrier, who was described as sharp-witted and affectionate. According to Charles' son, Francis, Polly always knew when her owner was planning a trip away because she would see the first signs of packing in his study and, as a result, become low-spirited. Darwin's other dog was a large black and white mixed-breed Retriever called Bob. Darwin's seminal book, *On the Origin of Species*, was published on this day in 1859.

25 NOVEMBER

Crab

On this day in 1487, Elizabeth of York was crowned Queen of England. She gives birth to Henry VIII whose second wife, Anne Boleyn, gives birth to the baby girl who becomes Elizabeth I — and so the first Elizabethan Age dawns. Dogs as domestic pets had become popular by this time, and it is reported that Elizabeth I had a little dog that went everywhere with her, though its name has been lost in the mists of time. One of the writers who flourished in the Elizabethan Age was William Shakespeare, who used dogs as symbols of loyalty and whose play *Two Gentlemen of Verona* features a dog called Crab.

Garcia

Garcia was an Australian Cattle Dog who belonged to Hollywood actor Owen Wilson, whose most famous dog film is *Marley & Me.* The duo, Owen and Garcia, were featured in a book about celebrities and their dogs called *Top Dogs and Their Pet*. Owen's film *Wedding Crashers* had just been released when photographer David Woo snapped the pair. He visited Owen at his Santa Monica home and asked the actor if he thought the dog would jump up for a photo. Owen, relaxed as ever, sauntered over to the fridge, took out a piece of turkey, which he held at head height, and Garcia leapt for it. In the dynamic photo, he is about 0.6 m (2 feet) up in the air. Owen also has a home on the Hawaiian Island of Maui, where the first ever European visitor was Captain James Cook, who landed there on this day in 1778.

Sirius

As a young man, Roman Emperor Marcus Aurelius was said to be inseparable from Sirius, his canine companion. In the night skies, Sirius is also called Alpha Canis Majoris, or the Dog Star. It is the brightest star in the night sky and you can see it by following the three stars that make up Orion's belt in a downwards direction — or, better still, download a stargazing app! On this day in AD 176 , Aurelius, who was Roman emperor from AD 161 to 180, made his son, Commodus, the Supreme Commander of the Roman legions.

Wolfie & Sasha

Percy is the name of the canine actor we see in the 2017 film *Paddington 2.* In the film, Percy plays Wolfie, the stray Irish Wolfhound whom Paddington befriends. Percy's human co-stars included Hugh Grant, Hugh Bonneville, Ben Whishaw, Brendan Gleeson, Sally Hawkins and Madeleine Harris. The first *Paddington* film was released on this day in 2014. Dog lover Hugh Bonneville has a dog called Sasha, and once posted a picture of the pooch out on a walk on International Dog Day with the caption, 'Sun's out, tongue's out!'

29 NOVEMBER

Blumer & Venom

Blumer and Venom are the names of the dogs in an Edmund Ward Gill oil on canvas painting titled *Two Dogs, Called 'Blumer' and 'Venom'*, which currently hangs in the National Trust property Attingham Park. Gill was a mainly landscape painter whose work was exhibited at the Royal Academy from 1842 to 1886. His two brothers, William Ward Gill and George Reynold Gill, were also painters. Edmund was born on this day in 1820.

30 NOVEMBER

Puffy

Border Terrier Slammer plays Puffy, the dog lead in the film *There's Something About Mary,* which also starred dog lover Ben Stiller, alongside Cameron Diaz. In real life, Ben, who celebrates his birthday today, has three dogs, one of whom is a rescue. Cameron is a dog lover too and has one more than Ben because she shares four dog 'kids', several of which are rescues, with musician husband Benji Madden.

DECEMBER

1 DECEMBER

Jet, Duke, Hector, Nellie, Dot, Juno, Shep, Grim & Otis

He was the 19th President of the United States and a former governor of Ohio – a predominantly rural state – so it is no surprise that Rutherford B. Hayes was a huge dog lover counting these nine in his dog family. Jet was a mixed breed, Duke an English Mastiff, Hector a Newfoundland, Dot a Cocker Spaniel, Grim a Greyhound and Otis a Miniature Schnauzer. Hayes, who installed the first telephone in the White House on this day in 1878, served from 1877 to 1881.

Marco

Some dogs can't stand to miss out on any fun, and this was certainly the case with Marco, a St Bernard mix belonging to English composer Ethel Smyth. The story goes that Smyth, studying music in Leipzig in the late 1880s, took Marco along with her to a rehearsal of the Brahms Piano Quintet in 1887, in the presence of the composer himself. No sooner had the musicians started than Marco, who had been settled down somewhere out of the way, burst into the room and knocked over a music stand. Thankfully, Brahms was reportedly a dog lover, and no harm was done. His 3rd Symphony in F had premiered with the Vienna Philharmonic Orchestra on this day four years earlier, in 1883.

Zep

Zep – short for Zeppelin – belongs to acting royalty, as he is Dame Vanessa Redgrave's little dog. Vanessa starred in the 2003 film *Good Boy!* – a science-fiction comedy based on the book *Dogs from Outer Space* by Zeke Richardson, and was the voice of The Greater Dane, who is the leader of Canid 3942 (Hubble) and the dogs. She also played Guinevere opposite Richard Harris's King Arthur in the 1967 musical film *Camelot*. The film followed the success of the Broadway show *Camelot*, which opened at the Majestic Theatre in New York on this day in 1960.

Teddy & Peanut

Cocker Spaniel Teddy moved to Pickle Cottage in January 2022, joining mum-of-four Stacey Solomon and her husband, Joe Swash, and the family dog, Peanut. Posting on her Instagram page to welcome Teddy, Stacey explained, 'We didn't pick him out, but we said we would take any dog suitable for young children and another dog.' She revealed that they were happy regardless of breed 'as long as he would be happy'. In 2010, Stacey was crowned Queen of the Jungle on this day as part of the tenth series of ITV's *I'm A Celebrity... Get Me Out of Here!*

Balloon Dog

The artwork that smashed all the records for the sale of art by a living artist was *Balloon Dog* by American artist Jeff Koons which, in 2013, sold at a Christie's New York auction for a staggering $58 million. The giant stainless steel, balloon-style sculpture of an orange dog stands 3.6 m (12 feet) high and was part of the artist's 1994 *Celebration* series. 'When I made "Balloon Dog" I wanted to make a piece that reflected the joy of celebrating a birthday or a party,' the artist explained. On this day in 1766, a London auctioneer called James Christie held his first sale.

6 DECEMBER

Lola, Pat & Mr Shakes

Actor and activist Kristen Bell has rehomed multiple dogs over the years, including Lola, Pat, Sadie and Mr Shakes. She currently has two rescues, Frank and Whiskey, and makes no secret of her preference for rehoming from rescue centres. 'I adore dogs, I think they're nature's natural antidepressants,' she once said. The *Frozen* star is also a dog foster carer, looking after rescue animals between homes. *Frozen* was released on this day in 2013.

7 DECEMBER

Mushroom

Mushroom played the dog Barney (also referred to as Woof-Woof by Gizmo) in the hit film *Gremlins*. He is the pet dog of the Peltzer family and, in the original film commentary, the director, Steven Spielberg, stated he was one of the best actors in the film. *Gremlins* was released in the UK on this day in 1984. Mushroom also played Gypsy in Stan Winston's supremely spooky *Pumpkinhead* and, though he only did a pair of pictures in his regrettably fleeting career, Mushroom nonetheless remains a much beloved animal actor among 1980s fright film afficionados.

8 DECEMBER

Mari and her puppies

Rescue dog Mari was a Shiba Inu who not only survived the 2004 earthquake in Japan – along with her three puppies – but also helped her owners get rescued. Unless you live in Japan, you may not know about the film *A Tale of Mari and Three Puppies*, which was released on this day in 2007 and which tells the story of the loyal little dog and how she survived two weeks under the rubble of an earthquake after her human family had been rescued. They were evacuated but came back two weeks later to find Mari still alive and with three plump and healthy puppies.

9 DECEMBER

Diva, Tessie & Chi Chi

Actress Lily Tomlin is a lifelong animal lover and often talks about the dogs she has shared her life with when she's being interviewed – these include Chi Chi, a Corgi mix, who was the family pet when she was growing up and, later on in life, Diva, the Doberman and Tessie, the Terrier, who she lived with as an adult. Lily says actors actually have a lot to learn from dogs, adding, 'Dogs just want to love their people, and actors need to love their audience. Dogs have all the empathetic qualities that a good actor should have.' In real life, Lily is married to the writer, director and producer Jane Wagner. The couple married in 2013. On this day in 2017, the Marriage Amendment Bill received royal assent and came into effect in Australia.

10 DECEMBER

Carlos & Leon

Carlos is a cool name for a Chihuahua and this little rescue landed squarely on all four paws when he moved into his new home with Hollywood actor and lifelong animal advocate Matt Damon, who played Linus Caldwell in the 2004 heist film *Ocean's Twelve*. Filmed in France, Italy, Monaco, the Netherlands and the United States, the film was the second in the franchise and was released on this day in that year. In another film, *We Bought a Zoo,* Matt plays the dad who moves his family – including a Beagle called Leon – to Dartmoor to do just that!

11 DECEMBER

Bonne, Nonne & Ponne

The French King who built the lavish Palace of Versailles didn't just make the place dog-friendly – he made it dog heaven! Louis XIV adored and doted on his three little dogs, Bonne, Nonne and Ponne, and in 1702 even commissioned a portrait of the trio from the French artist Alexandre-François Desportes. The painting hung in the antechamber to the King's suite at Marly and you can still see the early sketches for the piece in the collections of the Musée de la Chasse et de la Nature in Paris. Such was the King's devotion to this trio, he took personal care of their needs and frequently left important council meetings to check in on them. On this day in 1792, the decision was taken to put Louis on trial for treason, signalling the start of the French Revolution.

12 DECEMBER

Widget & Sugar

Supermodel turned businesswoman Cindy Crawford has two Maltese-Yorkie mixes called Widget and Sugar. On this day in 1991, the model married actor Richard Gere in a low-key Las Vegas ceremony, where the couple used aluminium foil for makeshift wedding rings. At 26, Cindy was 17 years younger than Richard, and had been dating him for four years after meeting him at a barbecue party hosted by photographer Herb Ritts.

13 DECEMBER

Pablo

Tibetan terrier Pablo is well used to mixing with the literary set and, as the pampered pooch of actress Helena Bonham Carter, has even attended the famous Hay Literary Festival. Helena made her name playing a young Edwardian socialite called Lucy Honeychurch in the Merchant Ivory period drama *A Room with a View*, which was released on this day in 1985. When Helena split from her long-term partner Tim Burton, she said it was her dogs who helped her over her heartbreak.

Poppy & Sam

Dog lover Jon Gopsill was enjoying a beach walk in Somerset, England when his dogs, Poppy and Sam, led him to something unusual in the sand. What the Spaniels found was the fossil of a 190-million-year-old Ichthyosaur – minus its head! John, an amateur archaeologist, said he often takes his dogs to the rocks, where the skeleton was found, when the tide goes out because they like playing there. The prehistoric find – which palaeontologists nicknamed 'Poppy' after one of the dogs – is 1.65 m (5 ft 5 in) long and was acquired by the Museum of Somerset so it could be put on display locally.

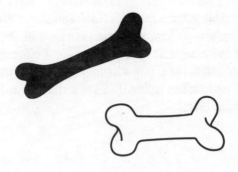

15 DECEMBER

Bothie

An adventurous Jack Russell called Bothie is the only dog to have ever travelled to both the North and South Poles as a member of a very prestigious British expedition team. Bothie was owned by the British explorer Sir Ranulph Fiennes and his wife, Ginny, and so travelled with the team on the two-year-long circumpolar transglobal expedition. The British adventurer led a team that left Greenwich in London in September 1979 and arrived at the South Pole on this day in 1980.

16 DECEMBER

Molly, Horace & Daisy

On this day in 2014, horror writer Stephen King introduced the world (via Twitter) to his new Corgi, Molly, who quickly gained on online reputation for her hilarious antics – because when he's not busy writing blockbuster books and scripts, the author, who is clearly besotted with his dog, is busy sharing details of Molly's latest capers. King has had many Corgis over the years and has even featured Corgi characters in his books, including Horace in *Under the Dome* and Daisy in *The Regulators*.

17 DECEMBER

Santa's Little Helper

Yup, it's none other than the Simpsons' family dog, who makes his first appearance in an episode called 'Simpsons Roasting on an Open Fire', which first aired on this day in 1989. The dog is a Greyhound who becomes a local hero in the episode 'Stop, or my Dog will Shoot!' in which he rescues Homer and gets enrolled in the Police Dog Academy, where he teams up with Lou to become a crime-busting duo. Santa's Little Helper is also known as No. 8 (his former racing number).

18 DECEMBER

Hulk

When Argentinian footballer Lionel Messi returned home after helping his team to win their third World Cup trophy in 2022, it was his dog, Hulk, who was serenaded by fans in an affectionate tribute which went viral after being posted on TikTok, where it has had over a million views. The final, which was beamed across the world on this day, saw Argentina beat France in penalties after a 3-3 score. Veteran footballer Messi had scored seven goals throughout the tournament, making him the second highest scorer after France's Kylian Mbappé. Gentle giant Hulk is a French Mastiff.

19 DECEMBER

TG

Happy Birthday to dog lover and TV presenter Richard Hammond, who was born on this day in 1969. When Richard famously had a near-fatal crash in 2006, he and his wife, Mindy, rehomed the Labradoodle, which Mindy described as being just like a 'woolly bear,' and the loyal dog stayed by Richard's size throughout his recovery. Despite not really being a fan of cars, TG became the programme's mascot when Richard came back to work.

Cassie & Max

The late singer-songwriter and guitarist John Denver loved dogs and named his two Cassie and Max. And if you're ever in Aspen, Colorado with a dog, you can be sure of a great walk at the John Denver Sanctuary, which runs adjacent to the popular Rio Grande hiking trail. Composer John wrote many hits for other artists, including the song 'Leaving on a Jet Plane', which topped the Billboard 100 chart on this day in 1969. John had originally called the song 'Babe I Hate to Go', but the title was changed for the folk trio Peter, Paul and Mary, who had formed in New York in 1961 and who were key players in the revival that decade of American folk music.

Arthur

On this day in 2005, superstar Elton John and his partner, David Furnish, cemented their relationship with a civil ceremony in which Elton's best friend, Arthur, was Best Man. Arthur was a Cocker Spaniel who had been given to Elton for his 56th birthday and when the dog passed away in 2018 at the age of 14, Elton announced his passing during a Las Vegas concert, where he said he was heartbroken and sang 'Don't Let the Sun Go Down on Me' for his dear four-legged companion.

22 DECEMBER

Marquis

Marquis was the little French Poodle who inspired the classical composer Chopin to write a piano piece called 'Waltz of the Puppy', which became better known as the 'Minute Waltz'. The little dog in question was Marquis, a pampered poodle who belonged to Chopin's then mistress, Amantine-Lucile-Aurore Dupin de Francueil, the French writer who assumed a male pen name, George Sand, in order to get published. It is said that Chopin was watching the little Poodle spinning around when the idea for the waltz came to him. Miss Violet and Miss Scarlett are two Poodles spoiled rotten by their dog mum, and another musical talent, Barbara Streisand. She is one of the bestselling female artists of all time, and her musical film *Hello Dolly* was released on this day in 1969.

23 DECEMBER

Dinks

She clearly has a way with words – and amusing dog names – because Dinks is the name that the first woman to be Poet Laureate, Carol Ann Duffy, chose for her dog. The Scottish-born poet and playwright, who celebrates her birthday today, was Poet Laureate from 2009 until her resignation in 2019. Her work is studied on the schools' curriculum in the UK and she is currently professor of contemporary poetry and the creative director of the Writing School at Manchester Metropolitan University.

24 DECEMBER

Nemo

Black Labrador-Griffon cross Nemo did his bit for his rescue dog pals at Christmas when he appeared in a video that started with the caption, 'My story begins with abandonment... like me, 100,000 animals are abandoned every year in France.' Nemo's owners are Emmanuel and Brigitte Macron, who rehomed him from a rescue centre in 2017. Nemo's video urges people to adopt rather than shop for a dog, but also urges potential owners to rehome with awareness of the commitment a dog needs from them.

Newton

On Christmas Day in 2020, Shonda Rhimes' Regency drama *Bridgerton* premiered on Netflix, and when the second season came along in March 2022, the streaming channel announced that the show had the highest opening weekend viewing figures of any English language TV series, with audiences viewing a staggering 193 million hours. That means millions of people worldwide were introduced to Newton, who is the pampered Corgi pooch belonging to the character Kate Sharma/Lady Kate Bridgerton (played by Simone Ashley). Newton is played by Austin, who has won multiple awards at Crufts.

26 DECEMBER

Rory, Snoozer, Tinkle, Jumper & Scarf

These five dogs are the stars of the Christmas film *Santa's Little Yelpers,* and so if you're in need of a puppy 'fix' this Boxing Day, this could be an option to explore. They are a tribe of Golden Retrievers who have been left by their bankrupt two-legged owners, who skip town without their family pet and her litter of puppies. In this heart-warming tale, the dogs are befriended by a boy who has run away from home and, together, they manage to stop a bank robbery and find a loving family who want to rehome them all. Pass the Christmas box of tissues...

27 DECEMBER

Wessex

Wessex belonged to the author Thomas Hardy, who loved his dog so much he even wrote two poems about him. Wessex was a Fox Terrier and lived with Thomas and his second wife, Florence, at the couple's Dorchester home. 'Wessie' even had royal connections because he was related to Caesar, Edward VII's Terrier. One of the Hardy family's friends was the dramatist and novelist J.M. Barrie (creator of Peter Pan) who would tell the story of how Hardy once showed him a letter from a company that had presented him with a radio. They were initially delighted to find out he liked it, only to learn from someone else that the radio was, in fact, acquired for Wessex. On this day in 2022, the Hardy Tree in the St Pancras Old Church burial grounds fell down. Thomas Hardy, who had trained as an architect, had once been assigned the task of clearing the grounds to make way for the railway service that would arrive there.

28 DECEMBER

Puey, Penny, Pearl, Pebbles, Petey and Pepper

These six dogs belong to celebrity couple John Legend and Chrissy Teigen. The dog-mad couple, who like to rehome rescue dogs and who will be celebrating John's birthday today, clearly have a thing about giving their dogs names starting with the letter 'P' since their two previous dogs were called Puddy and Pippa. Singer-songwriter John has sold over half a million albums since releasing his debut album, *Get Lifted*, at the end of 2004.

29 DECEMBER

Percy

Percy the Pug (voiced by Danny Mann) is a major character in the 1998 Disney film and sequel *Pocahontas II: Journey to a New World.* Formerly the Pug belonging to Governor Ratcliffe, the little dog becomes the pet and a friend of Pocahontas. While the first film dealt with the arrival of the first British settlers in Jamestown, this sequel is an animated musical that focuses on our heroine's journey to England to negotiate for peace between the two nations. In real life, on this day in 1607, Pocahontas is said to have successfully pleaded for the life of the explorer John Smith, who had established the first English settlement in Jamestown and whom tribal leaders wanted to execute.

30 DECEMBER

Buttercup, Fraak & Spotte

As a boy growing up in Texas, Mike Nesmith, one of the members of the 1960s band the Monkees, had a dog he named Buttercup. A dog lover his whole life, Fraak and Spotte were Nesmith's dogs when the band recorded 'Gonna Buy Me A Dog', which was all about how a hapless guy who had just been dumped was going to get a dog to get him over his heartbreak. According to fanzine *Monkee Spectacular*, Spotte the dog was found wandering in the desert near Mike's home and was given to him by some of the people working for him at that time. This song was the final track on the Monkees' debut studio album, which was released in 1966. Mike was born on this day in Texas in 1942.

31 DECEMBER

Duke, Chandler & Cali

These three belong to the two-time Olympic medal champion gymnast Gabby Douglas, who says her natural approach to diet and exercise is something she extends to her dogs. Gabby says the dogs love to exercise with her when she's training too. 'It's so funny because sometimes when I do my workout, [the dogs] literally tag along. Like I love to run the stairs, I love to run laps around my house, and so they'll just follow me and it's honestly a great thing because the more active that we can keep them, the better.'

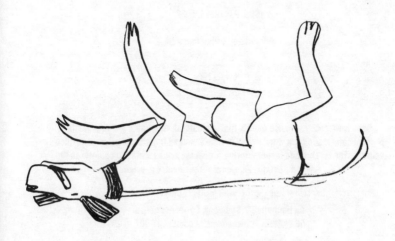

First published in 2023 by Welbeck.
This edition published in 2024 by Welbeck.
An Imprint of HEADLINE PUBLISHING GROUP

Design and layout © 2023 Carlton Books Limited
Text © 2023 Carlton Books Limited

Produced under license from Battersea Dogs Home Limited to go towards supporting
the work of Battersea Dogs & Cats Home (registered charity no 206394). For all
licensed products sold by Welbeck across their Battersea range, Welbeck will donate
a minimum of £20,000 plus VAT in royalties to Battersea Dogs Home Limited, which
gives its profits to Battersea Dogs & Cats Home.
battersea.org.uk

Text by Susan Clark except 9, 14, 29 Jan, 16 March, 24 April, 30, 31 May, 14 June, 22
July, 2, 3, 16 Aug, 12, 19 Oct, 2 Dec by Carlton Books Limited

Cataloguing in Publication Data is available from the British Library

ISBN 9781035425532

Printed and bound in the UK

MIX
Paper | Supporting
responsible forestry
FSC® C104740

Headline's policy is to use papers that are natural, renewable and recyclable
products and made from wood grown in well-managed forests and other controlled
sources. The logging and manufacturing processes are expected to conform to the
environmental regulations of the country of origin.

HEADLINE PUBLISHING GROUP
An Hachette UK Company, Carmelite House
50 Victoria Embankment, London EC4Y 0DZ

www.headline.co.uk
www.hachette.co.uk